STRETCHED THIN

Brady and Brett Nichols

ISBN: 0692789197
ISBN 13: 9780692789193

A mosaic of two brothers' lives...

"The Child is father of the Man."

William Wordsworth

BRADY
Irish Spring

Getting in trouble as a little kid sucks. Getting in trouble when you lived with the Old Man was a whole other level of suckiness. Getting in trouble with the Old Man for something that you didn't even do was unbearable.

Our elementary school had the 'riders' and the 'walkers.' The riders would have to organize and form lines when that last bell rang at the end of the day. They had to follow directions from the teachers until they boarded stuffy buses. Then they had to sit on the buses and follow more rules set by the bus drivers. I knew this because every once in a while I would go on a miserable bus ride to Seb's house across the river. Brett, Charlie, Bruce, Donny, and I were walkers. We got to bolt right when the bell rang. We would run out to the playground, wait for each other, and then start our walk back to the neighborhood. I won't exaggerate and say that we had to walk home eight miles in four feet of snow or anything like that, but it was a long walk. I looked forward to it every day. We got to talk about stuff, mess around, and just unwind from a day of constantly being told where to sit, what to write, and to be quiet. There were great climbing trees on the way home that we would sit in some days. We would have milkweed fights in the fall when the ripe pods would explode after they hit someone in the head.

One day walking home, Charlie used the word 'shit' in a sentence. It was the first time in early elementary school that any one of us kids had used a swear word around each other.

"Shit," she blurted out as she accidentally busted the stick from which she was trying to peel the bark. She used the swear so casually. She didn't say it after getting a painful splinter or anything. She was just walking peeling this stick and it broke. We would hear the adults say words like that all the time, but we had never even come close to saying them until now.

Charlie never even looked up from peeling that stick.

"Today was a shitty day." She said it again as if it were no big deal.

We didn't want to seem immature by acting shocked so we kept our mouths closed. But inside I couldn't believe she could say that, and I knew the other guys were surprised too. She not only blurted it twice but said it two more times by the time we reached her house. It was as if she just learned the word and kept saying it in order to experience how its pronunciation would feel on her tongue. Regardless, we all just walked home as usual, talked about what we normally talked about, and pretended that we never heard Charlie say 'shit' four times total.

Two days later my brother and I were at Mimi's house waiting for my mother to finish her shift and The Old Man to get back from his short lived job. When both my parents arrived we would all drive home like one big happy family.

When the Old Man arrived before my mother got dropped off by her nursing friends, he made a beeline for me. Bad sign: I knew something was wrong. Of course, being at Mimi's house working on artwork and just doing simple stuff with my brother all afternoon, I had no idea why the Old Man would have a beef with me this particular day.

"Brady, come over here," he said in a tone that made my blood turn icy.

"Yeah?" I responded sheepishly while trying to 'come over' but also to stay a decent distance away. The distance had to be the perfect amount: to actually do what he said, but enough away so that he couldn't grab me.

"Let me ask you something. Come here," he commanded.

Crap. Now I had to get close. I never liked to be that close to him - ever.

I just stood and looked at him. His black hair was slicked back, and his-just-as black eyes were now staring right at me.

"Yeah?" I was shaking, just a tiny bit.

"Did you swear the other day?" he asked.

I had no idea what he was asking. It was like he was speaking another language. I was in third grade and had never sworn in my life.

"What?" I heard the question, but I didn't know what he was talking about.

"You heard me. Did you cuss the other day?" he repeated as his anger grew.

"No."

"Don't lie to me. You know I hate liars." His voice was insistent.

"No. I didn't."

"Well, you said 'shit.' That is what I hear." Now his hands clenched both my arms. They could easily wrap all the way around my skinny biceps. His grasp always made them feel like toothpicks.

"I didn't say that."

"Someone said you did, walking home from school the other day." Then the memory of Charlie swearing the other day flashed into my head. But why would he think that I did?

"It was someone else," I said. And for a moment I had a little bit of hope that he would believe me. I didn't cuss. Charlie did four times.

The flickering flame of hope was there one moment and completely snuffed out the next. It was like the Old Man just licked his fingers and pinched it out like he had so many times before.

"Now you know I hate liars," he growled as he pulled me toward the bathroom.

"And you know that I don't like potty mouths," he continued as he closed the door behind us.

"You need to understand that you can't talk like that."

"But I didn't!" I pleaded.

He shook me and tears started running down my face.

"Don't lie!" He was sitting on the closed toilet staring straight into my eyes.

"Now you need to take your medicine like a man."

He took a bar of Irish Spring from Mimi's bathroom sink -- the kind that had the green and the white swirls. He broke it in half and said, "Eat this."

He jammed the first half in my mouth.

"Now chew it and don't spit any out."

I continued to cry. The taste was awful, but I chewed as I was told. That was the easy part.

"Now swallow." That was the hard part. I tried to swallow, but it made me gag. He put his huge paw of a hand across my mouth and demanded that I not spit out anything.

As my scrawny eight year old body shook, cried, chewed, swallowed and gagged, he said, "Good boy."

"Now this one." He held up the second half.

While I broke up the last bit of Irish Spring in my mouth, I could hear my mother pounding and yelling on the other side of the door. The Old Man simply ignored her protests (as usual). He took his sweet time, pretending that he didn't hear her.

He did not get up until he was certain that I got most of the second chunk down. Then he tousled my red hair as he went to open the door, and walked past my mother as she rushed in towards me. She muttered, "You are the biggest asshole" under her breath.

"Are you all right?" she asked as I retched into the sink. Bits of green and white launched from my stomach in protest. I shook uncontrollably. My mother kept asking me if I was ok, but I could not respond. My mouth felt numb. Even my brain felt numb at this point. I really couldn't comprehend fully what had happened. I didn't lie. I didn't say 'shit.' What I did know, and what was crystal clear at that moment, however, is that I had downed a nasty bar of Irish Spring.

It took a while to wash out my mouth with water. My mom hovered over me trying to help me do a task that only I really could do. She rubbed my back and cried a little bit with me.

"Are you o.k.?" she asked for the tenth time. When my mouth started to get feeling back, I told her that I was ok. She wiped the tears off my cheeks and called the Old Man some more choice names, names that I am pretty sure that if I had said would earn me more bars of soap.

I finally gathered myself and walked out of the bathroom with my mother's arms around me. And still, after using seemingly gallons of water to flush my mouth out, I still had a faint taste of Irish Spring.

Ironically, one word came to mind at that moment: shit.

BRETT
The Piano Man

While growing up, it was always fun when the family got to-gether, especially when it was without my dad or as Brady called him: the Old Man. Our family wasn't big, but being sur-rounded by my mother's side of the family, cousins from dad's side and seeing everyone laugh, playing horseshoes or sitting by the bonfire telling stories was the best. I never wanted some of those long summer nights at The Camp to end. All the kids would have their mouse traps ready (the old wooden ones slathered with peanut butter and set around the inside of The Camp). Everyone had their favorite spot: the fireplace was a good one, the crack by the stairs, or almost any exterior wall where there was some large piece of furniture. We would argue about who was going to get a mouse by morning. It was a ritual every night: as if it were Christmas when the kids would come downstairs to see if Santa left presents at the crack of dawn. My brother and I had our personal rivalry of course. We had to compare who got the biggest rodent. Some nights you would hear the traps snap, and we would sit there wondering whose it could be, but we were too lazy to check until morning.

Instead, all the kids would remain upstairs in the dark telling jokes or scary stories. We stayed up giggling for as long as our eyelids could stay open. One night, it was way past midnight, and we were all on edge from our oldest cousin, Ivan, telling us horror stories. Off in the distance we could hear a voice outside.

"Shhhhh. You hear that?" someone said.

It was so dark up in the attic that you could not see a hand in front of your face.

"Listen."

When we got everyone quiet and listened real hard, we could hear a man traveling through the night.

"What the heck is that?"

"Shut up!"

As we listened closer, it seemed to be a male voice singing. Now we were totally hooked, and no one was saying a word. The man's voice slowly got closer and closer, until we could make out the words:

"And he's quick with a joke or to light up your smoke
But there's someplace that he'd rather be..."

After a moment the unfamiliar bled into the familiar.

"Well I am sure that I could be a movie star,
If I could get out of this place....."

Not only did my brother and I now recognize the lyrics from Billy Joel, but we immediately knew the singer.

"Let's go! That is Uncle Phil!" Brady and I yelled almost in tandem.

"Are you guys sure that is him?" the others said, not convinced that we were telling the truth. First scary stories and now this haunting song being sung in the dead of night in the woods: skepticism was high.

"Are you sure you know that is him?"

Brady and I let the other cousins continue their reluctant chatter as we bolted through the door. As my brother and I stood at the corner of the porch and looked out at the road, we could now hear our Uncle Phil singing the song clearly. It was so dark that we could barely see his figure staggering down the road.

> *"And the piano, it sounds like a carnival*
> *And the microphone smells like a beer*
> *And they sit at the bar and put bread in my jar*
> *And say, "Man, what are you doin' here?"*

When he got close to the driveway Brady and I ran over.

"Uncle Phil! Uncle Phil!"

"Are those my boys 'Red Cloud' and the 'Wild Child'?" he shot back with a grin. Those were the two nicknames he gave us. Brady was 'Red Cloud' from the naughty boy in the movie *Ransom of Red Chief* and I was 'Wild Child', well, because I was wild.

Under the bright moonlight we could finally see all the details of our Uncle's face as we ran over to him.

"Come see your Uncle," he said in a lazy voice laced with beer. As we got closer we realized he was banged up. His clothes were torn. He had scrapes and bruises all over his arms and hands.

"What happened?" we asked.

"Bike trouble," he said with a smile.

His injuries did not stop him from giving us a big bear hug. He put his arms around us and walked us towards The Camp. By now everyone was up waiting for the 'mysterious' Piano Man. My mom stared at him with a stern expression as she slowly shook her head, but didn't say a word because she wanted to keep the smiles on our faces.

The morning of the next day we walked out with Uncle Phil to the end of the dirt road to find his motorcycle all smashed up.

However, that night, before we went back up to bed, we convinced him to tell us a couple of scary stories because, after all, he was the Master Story Teller. Brady and I were in our glory. Here was the guy that we bragged about to all our cousins, and now he was here telling us stories in the middle of the night.

After he was done and my mom shooed us upstairs, we laid under the covers letting the long night take over our dreams. I stayed awake for a few more minutes with a big grin on my face. A couple traps went off downstairs like fireworks off in the distance. As I closed my eyes I anticipated us all tiptoeing downstairs on 'christmas morning' to see our presents, and I could not help but hope that my trap had the biggest mouse.

BRADY
Stretched Thin

We lived in a crappy little house in Baldwinville, Massachusetts. My mother worked hard. She was a nurse at the local hospital. She worked during the days and the nursing home most nights after coming home for a bit. She made us something to eat when she got home and then constantly cleaned. She never sat down. She would mop the floors and dust the tables. She never stopped. Mimi would say, "Kathleen! You are going to have a heart attack." Considering the situation that we lived in, I always found it a bit odd that she would spend so much time cleaning after work. With the Old Man not making any money and making a mess of things all day, I always wondered what the point of mopping the floor three times a week was. Wouldn't she want to sit down for a couple minutes and take a rest? I had my chores. I vacuumed the carpets and tried to clean the bathrooms. She even vacuumed over what I had vacuumed earlier. I got mad and asked her why she cleaned over what I cleaned earlier?

She told me that it was all right; it 'calmed her.' I didn't even like doing the minimal chores I had. I just did them because I wanted to help my mother. I saw how hard she had it.

My mother's room was in the basement, and the carpet was always damp due to the bad drainage of the house. It was funny how my brother, my mother, and I knew where the water collected so we could tiptoe in certain areas and not get our feet wet. Once we were on her bed we called it the safety. We pulled up our legs and felt safe from the consistently wet carpet.

The Old Man often left for long periods of time and then showed up at home to make our lives miserable for a while. When he came back he brought a few gifts and was all nice for a day or two, but then it was back to business as usual. Business as usual was my mom working hard and The Old Man working hard at getting drunk. All he seemed to do was go out and come back staggering and then get nasty. He smacked us around if we got in his way or if we laughed too much. I always thought laughing was a good thing, just not around my father. Laughing was noise, and he hated noise. He said that we were 'meant to be seen not heard.' I sometimes listened on the playground to the laughter of the other kids and thought how good it sounded, all these kids laughing having a good time playing kickball and tag. I wondered what their houses were like. Everyone in our house had to tiptoe around in fear that The Old Man might snap. My mother called it walking on eggshells.

He busted up vases or anything he could get his hands on when he got into one of his raging fits. One time I thought about telling him that instead of busting up the lamp by the tv, he could just bring it to a pawn shop and get some money for it. That way instead of talking about the job that he never got he could at least actually have an income. One time he threw something through the t.v. which made no sense at all. He must have forgotten that the tv was the one thing in the house that seemed to pacify him. He laid on the couch watching that thing for hours.

One day in the fall when my father was back home for whatever reason, we stacked cord wood for the winter. He had this big black eye. He had it when he returned after being gone for a few weeks. It interested me and my brother as to how this person we feared so much who seemed near invincible could have a black eye.

"Dad, what happened to your eye?"

"What does it matter to you?" He barked.

"I was just wondering," I answered sheepishly.

I didn't want to push it too much for fear of myself ending up with a similar mark. There was a long pause before anything else was said. Then he picked up a big piece of wood and said, "I was backstabbed by your uncle."

Backstabbed. At first I did not understand how if one was stabbed he ended up with a black eye. It wasn't until years later that I figured out that my father was confronted in a bar by my mother's brother, Uncle Phil, about the bruises the Old Man was giving his sister. They went outside and had it out in the parking lot. I can't imagine two grown men beating the pulp out of each other in a parking lot. My father was a big man and my uncle was just as big. That must have been a sight to see. The next time I saw my uncle he didn't have a scratch on him. I have to admit, it made me smile inside a little.

Sometimes things got especially nasty when the Old Man was around for extended periods of time. He would drink and come home late waking everyone up intentionally. He'd walk in the house stumbling. He'd head straight to my mom's room while she was trying to get some rest for work the next morning. They'd fight. Stuff would crash. Sometimes the next day I woke up to see the house in disarray.

My brother and I stayed outside for as long as we could during such times. We didn't return home until we were certain that my mother was there. She was like a beacon of light that cut through his darkness. He did hit her hard, but she always seemed to get up, brush herself off and take care of Brett and me.

They say cats can fall out of a tree and always land on their feet. I knew this crazy boy down the block who flung his cat and it always landed perfectly. My mother was like that cat – she would always seem to land upright. She would hardly show the strain. Every once in a while I caught her in the bathroom sitting on the edge of the tub smoking a cigarette with the door closed. I knocked and she told me to come in. She didn't smoke regularly. So when I came in and saw her eyes all red and smoking like that, I knew she was stretched thin. She wouldn't try to hide the fact that she was smoking from me. She'd just tell me to come over and then put her arm around me. She'd start to cry. I felt bad. I felt like I was the reason she was crying. Yeah, she seemed upset initially, but she wasn't really crying until she put her arms around me.

"Everything is going to be all right," she'd say.

She always said stuff like that, but I knew it wasn't true. I never figured out if she was trying to convince me or trying to convince herself. Either way, my mom was always telling us that 'things were going to be o.k.' She was constantly trying to make things seem better than they really were. It was like the Wizard in Oz. However, Brett and I could see behind the curtain.

BRETT
Liar

In third grade I had a few friends with whom I spent most of my time, but Brian LaRossa and I were the class clowns. Brian would horse around in class like I did, except he was a straight A student and I was a straight C student. If it was cracking jokes in the class to try and get everyone to laugh or smacking each other with dusty erasers while "cleaning" them, he was always my partner when I got into mischief. One fall day in art class, we were doing watercolor. The class was pushing loaded brushes of pigment in order to create washes for skies, trees and bushes. Watching the colors bleed into one another producing a new hue was pretty cool and definitely held my attention for a while. In art class I was a little better than most. This was pretty satisfying because in other classes I would tend to struggle. I attribute my success in art to Mimi. Not only did Mimi have her own kiln but she had a whole studio that had painting supplies, ceramics, and other crafts that she was always willing to have us dabble with on a rainy day.

Towards the end of class the teacher asked if there were any volunteers to help clean up the painting supplies. My hand shot up because I loved getting out of the classroom for a bit. School and the constant sitting still in one desk just to move to another room and do the same thing all over again was such a drag. Brian was quick to follow my lead. He and I collected the palettes and brushes and cruised down to the bathroom to clean them off.

As we began to wash the brushes Brian flicked one a bit, and a little got on my arm. He giggled.

"Sorry."

"Yeah, right," I countered and then flicked a little on him.

Within seconds we were shoving the bristles of the brushes into the dirty trays and flicking them at each other. A quick flip at one another was followed by an insincere "whoops." Laughing the whole time, we reloaded brushes and began to duck and weave in order to not get the muddy pigment on us. Meanwhile, a third grader walked into the facilities and stopped dead in his tracks.

"You two are crazy," he said in disbelief. The battle stopped as the innocent bystander used the urinal but started right back up the second he exited.

Our inner clock notified us that we might want to get finished and return to class. We quickly wiped down the sinks and walls and headed back to class. When we walked into the classroom, all heads turned to Brian and me. I noticed that some kids' eyes went big, some just smiled and nudged one another, but Mrs. Moran gasped.

"Brett and Brian, what in the world happened to you?" The class erupted in laughter.

"We were cleaning the trays and a couple slipped," I responded.

Mrs. Moran just moved on and got the class focused on the next task.

She casually pulled us aside when the class got busy again, "Now, boys what a mess you have made of yourselves. The paint will come off in the wash, but still this looks a little more than just spilled paint."

She awkwardly paused to see if we wanted to add anything. It did not take me long to understand that the pause adults give you to 'explain yourself' is best used looking at your feet. In my experience, the more I said the worse things got.

After school my brother saw some of the remains of paint in my hair, face, and clothes.

"You're dead when Mom and Dad see you," he commented.

As we walked home I thought of the lines I would use. I decided it was going to be very similar to what I used for Mrs. Moran: I was helping clean up in class and a few trays slipped. It seemed like a great plan.

The second my mom laid eyes on me she flipped.

"What in the world did you do to your new school clothes?" she said through multiple sighs.

I restated my party line, and she jumped all over it.

"Brett you and that kid are always into something, and when your father comes home you are in deep trouble!" she threatened.

She was so mad that the instant he walked through the door she filled him in on my debacle. Mom didn't even let the guy loosen up and relax after work. She just wound him up and set him loose on me. When we were real little my dad didn't seem so bad. In the early years he worked for stretches of time, and some stints on Seven Grove Street even could be construed as normal. He certainly got worse as the years passed. However, the thing that remained constant was his ability to get more and more wound up as he yelled. The more he spoke, the angrier he got. Unfortunately, I was too little and too dumb to realize that the more I told the story and the more I veered from the truth, the more crimson his face would get. He was so pissed off before my story ended that I was already shaking. He asked me to repeat my version as if he didn't hear it the first time. He wanted to me to speak clearer so he could get things straight in his mind.

"Bullshit! You think I am going to believe you and that clown dropped the trays!" he interrupted my defunct second version.

"You liar!"

"You know what I hate more than anything? A liar!" He answered his own question. My father many times had expressed his contempt for lying. I had lived through the many promises that he broke. I had witnessed the plethora of straight-up deceptions he employed. However, if someone was dishonest with him he would completely flip out.

He carried on about 'you're only as good as your word' or 'do you take me as some fool' as he grabbed my arm, dragged me downstairs, and beat the crap out of me. I screamed at every connection that landed on my back and hind end.

When I returned to my room I will never forget my brother's face. He had this look as if he was just happy to see me alive. After he exhaled a big sigh of relief he said, "you are an idiot. When are you going to learn?"

"What? I was just painting," I calmly said through the throbbing I felt on the surface of my skin, not wanting to show my brother the pain I felt.

There got to a point early in my childhood, before my father started getting really nasty, that I would do silly stuff and not worry about the consequences. The risk seemed to outweigh the reward. The fun of the moment made the future appear as a distant, hazy, mirage that was not my concern. After all I could just stare at my feet when I could think of nothing else.

BRADY
Charlie

C harlie lived down the hill from us. She was in my grade, and I felt like I knew her since the day I was born. She was the first girl that I had a crush on. I am certain she was the first girl all the boys in the neighborhood had crushes on. It wasn't like she was the prettiest girl in the class, but she was just different than all the other girls, and she was much more developed. She was the first girl to make the Little League team with the boys. Shoot, the first year that I could try out for the Little League team, she made it and I didn't. I will never forget when the coaches posted the names of the kids who made teams in the hallway at school. Everyone gathered around to see the team they were on. I was not on any team list, and Charlie was on the Tigers. For the next couple years I was resigned to watching my brother and her play.

"Just try out again next year Brady," Ben said as he patted me on the back.

I knew there would not be a next year for me. Not being on one of the lists just reaffirmed that I sucked and I was not about to go through rejection the following season. I never tried out again.

Charlie was the only girl amongst seven brothers who were mostly older. So it is no wonder she was good at all the sports. Despite her petite stature, she could play football with us and score. I watched games where she would hit a couple homers in Little League. She could run with the fastest and even fight with some of the best. If you liked her and showed it, her older brothers would usually kick your ass. I am not talking about just a couple slaps. I am talking about beat-your-ass-and-leave-you-lying-on-the-ground.

So even if I did like her, I was not about to announce it. Even the day she took soapstone and wrote C.D. plus B.N. on the road, I stood above her and rubbed it out with my foot. She scooched down the road a little more, and wrote it once more and I scratch it out again. She did it about ten times while looking up at me smiling. I rubbed it out each time. There was always a little part of her doing stuff like that which made me wonder if she really liked me or if she was just messing with me. Why would she ever like a skinny, scrawny, red headed kid who didn't make the baseball team? I was not about to take a chance of showing any interest and getting the big brother beat down. There were lots of stories of boys looking at her a certain way and just getting brutishly smacked by Ronnie or Steve.

Her brothers protecting her so much was ironic because she could take care of herself pretty darn well from what I saw. Every kid who knew Charlie knew that she had no problem getting in people's faces if they offended her somehow. The guys on the block would just laugh when clueless boys tried to challenge her.

Our cousin Ivan was one of those boys. Ivan did not come over often, but when he did, it was not fun. He was older than I was, and he would spend most of his time trying to act like a tough guy, pushing my brother and me around, telling us how to do things. Brett and I tried to remain cool because he was our cousin, but he annoyed us. Ivan had to always be right even when he was wrong. I also hated that when he visited, his mother would bring his old clothes. Because I was the oldest and 'closest in age' to him, I had to wear them. His pants were too big and nothing ever fit right on me.

On one of these unpleasant visits, we went to play football at the park with Ivan and some of the neighborhood kids. Charlie showed up. Ivan of course noticed right away. When she asked to play, we all said, "no problem." But in typical ignorant and arrogant-boy fashion, Ivan tried to show he was the coolest by showing 'this girl' that he was better than she was.

"Heck no," Ivan cut in.

This was one of those gratifying times that the rest of us got to sit back and watch the show.

"Why not?" Charlie asked, already getting pissed.

"Cause, we are not going to play football with a girl."

That is when Brett and a few others tried to help old Ivan out a bit by telling him that Charlie was actually really good, and she played with them in Little League too. Ivan was not having any of it.

"I am not playing football with some girl," he repeated. Ivan had this smirk on his face thinking he was superior just because he was a male and taller or something.

Brett and I looked at each other with grins. It was on.

Charlie was really heated now. She stormed right over to him and got in his face.

"I am probably better than you!"

"I don't think so," Ivan said with a dismissive tone. He spoke to her as if she were just some little pest buzzing around bothering him. Big mistake.

While Ivan and Charlie stood toe to toe eyeing each other up and down, she sent a right uppercut straight to his stomach. His legs gave way, and he buckled to the ground. Ivan didn't make a sound for a while. We all started laughing. After Ivan laid on the ground and curled up into a ball, he started gasping and kind of moaning. With the wind totally knocked out of his body, he struggled to catch his breath. As all the boys in the neighborhood laughed and pointed at Ivan, Charlie just stood there waiting with her fists clenched. I think she wanted Ivan to get back up, but he wouldn't. When Ivan finally got his breath the tears came. The more his tears came, the more our laughter flowed.

Since he wasn't brave enough to face her, we all turned away and headed to play football at the park. Brett and I let Ivan find his way back to our house on his own. I think by the time we came back from playing a couple games at the park, Ivan and his mom were gone.

"Ivan came back early from the park. Did everything go all right boys?" My mom casually asked.

Brett and I just smiled and shrugged. The thought of Charlie standing over Ivan with her balled fists hoping he would get up just made our day.

BRETT
Matchbox Cars

S ome summers my mom dropped Brady and me off at Mimi's every day so she could go to work. On those hot summer days we played in Mimi's basement where it was cool. She had a really old house, and the basement had a dirt floor and a kiln sitting in the middle for her ceramic projects. Brady and I built roads all over that dirt for our matchbox cars. That held my attention for a little while, but I usually ended up quitting to go run around outside. Most of the time I fumbled around waiting for the sun to come out, or trying to convince Brady to take a break so we could get on our bikes and hit some jumps. Brady, on the other hand, could stay down there all day if I didn't force him to come with me. He built extensive roads, pushed all the cars, made sound effects and created characters for each of the cars for hours. I never understood how he could get lost in his mind as he did. His imagination absorbed the chaos of our lives. He created games and storylines where he didn't need anyone. If I played it was only as a support role to his larger story. I got pissed because my characters never did or became some of the cool things his did. I almost always immediately protested.

"What the heck Brady! I want my car to fly."

"Why can't my guy go that fast?"

"Why do those those cars get to be in that gang?"

Looking back I understand why he never let me in all the way. It wasn't because he was pulling his 'big brother card,' which he did so many times; it was simply because he knew I couldn't last long in the game. Even if we were having a rare good time and not fighting, I still yearned to get outside and run around.

Brady always seemed to be on the outside looking in when we were kids. As he worried about me getting into trouble, I worried about him fitting in. He always seemed to be happy just doing his own thing. He had no problem running around with us and seemed happy doing it, but he also had this other side where he was just as content in his own little world. He tried out for Little League once, and when he didn't make it, he never tried again and consented to being on the other side of the fence cheering for me. The guys and I bugged him every year to try out again. He would have made it no problem after that initial year, but he was stubborn. He dug in his heels and always replied, "Hell no."

Part of the reason he kept himself peacefully in the fringes was because he just didn't seem to care about impressing people. I did crazy stuff a lot of times just to get people's attention. He, on the other hand, had an inner strength and was going to be himself regardless of what people thought.

Then I saw him run. For the first time, I saw a different side of my brother. He was always fast. Everyone on our block knew he was one of the fastest. When our school sponsored races against other grade levels, I took the front row seat because that is when I knew my brother was going to shine. Kids talked about the typical athletes like Denis or Ron as favored to win. But when it came to straight-up running, I put my money on Brady every time.

The gym teachers picked some of the fastest kids from all the gym classes. The event was hyped up. The boys talked smack about who was the fastest and who was going to kick ass. Brady never said a word, though the more sporty dudes in his grade paraded around like they were going to crush everyone.

"I am going to kill this."

"I am going to smoke you all."

Back and forth they went, puffing their chests out for a couple days before the big event. The rest of us lined around the school to cheer. I wanted to be towards the last bend so I could see the finish.

When the gym teacher shot the gun, the runners took off around the back side of the school. We heard cheering from the kids on the other side. I saw this kid Nolan come around the corner first. He was in my brother's grade. I kind of knew him: a quiet kid like my brother. He had one of those Star Wars lunch boxes. Five steps later came my brother, then a big gap and everyone else.

They just had to climb the last straight away and that was it.

Brady gained with every step. The kids from the back side of the school ran over to the front to see the finish. Everyone screamed.

It was a photo finish. They leaned into it so close that I couldn't even tell. The gym teacher pointed to Nolan and the crowd erupted. Tons of kids mobbed around him. My brother walked over to the side with his hands on his hips catching his breath as I walked over.

"Nice, man," I said with a slap on the back. "That was close."

"Yeah," Brady puffed with a big grin on his face. "That was cool."

I stood there looking at him. The school crowded Nolan asking him all sorts of questions and patted him on the back telling him how fast he was. Brady and I stood off to the side just chillin'. As the saying goes, no one remembers second place. The crowd just wanted a piece of the winner. My brother looked up at the sky and caught his breath. He looked so happy and seemed cool with second place. If I came that close to winning and didn't, I would be so salty. But Brady seemed calm and at ease with it.

"Great race man," I said one last time before walking away.

Brady ran through nearly every difficult obstacle in our lives. He never ran *away* from our trials, although there would be reason to. When I watched him finish I saw him smile. Running did something for Brady whether he did or didn't win. Like pushing his cars down those dirt roads in my Mimi's basement, running gave him a peaceful and safe place to be content. He ran for a purpose beyond competition.

BRADY
Pajama Feet

My brother and I were staying at Grandma Thelma's house, in Gardner, which was a town over from ours. She was the Old Man's mother. Mimi was my mom's mother, and we stayed with her all the time, but we barely saw the Old Man's side of the family. She was watching us for the evening while my mother went out. I didn't really like staying with the Old Man's mom. I had trouble seeing Grandma Thelma as my Grandma even though she was nice enough. Mimi had such a warm personality that she was the only Grandmother I wanted to be with. Furthermore, Grandma Thelma and Alvin, the Old Man's stepfather, were chain smokers so their house stunk, and now we were stuck there for hours.

After her night out, my mother tip-toed into the back room to wake us up to take us home. We didn't even get out of our pajamas with the feet on them. Half asleep we slipped on our winter coats and started toward the door to step into our boots. That is when the Old Man's voice snapped us right awake.

The Old Man was on the porch arguing with my Mom. He had not been around for a few weeks, and he showed up unexpectedly as my mother was about to bring us home. My mother, Grandma Thelma, and Alvin, blocked the door.

"Where are my boys?" he demanded. He was obviously drunk, and in the midst of a regular routine where he would show up, all messed up, and start acting crazy.

"Just go, I am bringing them home," my mother said.

By now my brother and I were near the front door peering out the window. Standing at the bottom of the flight of steps in a t-shirt in the middle of winter was the Old Man. My mother, Alvin, and Grandma stood on the top of the porch.

"I want to see them," the Old Man slurred. He then started to climb the stairs as Alvin came down to meet him.

"I don't think that is a good idea in this state," Alvin interjected and attempted to block the Old Man's path.

"Get the hell out of my way!" the Old Man barked, throwing Alvin down the stairs as he continued up to the women.

"You are not taking them!" Mom screamed as she attempted to block his way.

My brother and I stood inside wide eyed as the Old Man grabbed her and threw her aside almost taking out Grandma. He crashed through the door and scooped up my brother and me, marched us to his car and threw us in the back seat of the Green Hornet. As he slammed the rear door and got in the front seat, we could hear my mother and Grandma crying and yelling for him to bring us back. Mom got back on her feet and stormed down the porch steps running in pursuit of the Hornet. The Old Man threw the car in reverse and skidded away.

I looked out the back window and saw my mother reach the street too late because by then we were well down the block. We turned a corner and she was gone. My brother was real young, and I had my arms around him and he was quietly sobbing. Our toes dangled from the seat as we tried not to get our pajama feet in the slushy stuff on the floor mats.

"Goddamn teach her."

"Try and say when I can see my kids."

The Old Man just grumbled sentences and cursed to himself. He never addressed us shivering in the back seat. He just went on about how he was going to teach my mother a lesson. Recognizing the state that he was in, I started calculating: left turn, another left turn, now a right turn and going for a little longer. I tried to look out into the dark city passing by to figure out where we were because I had no idea where we were going. We were moving fast, it was dark out, and we didn't spend a lot of time in Grandma's city.

We had been driving for a little while when the car came to an abrupt halt. We just sat idle for a minute or two. The Old Man grumbled some more about my mother and a bunch of other things I didn't understand.

"Get out," he said without looking back. It was the first time he addressed us during the whole trip.

We didn't move. We were on some abandoned road with some closed-down businesses. It didn't seem like any sort of destination.

"I said, get out!" he barked.

"Where are we?" I asked.

"Just get the hell out!" he yelled. That got us moving. I grabbed Brett and we got out of the Green Hornet and stood on the curb in our pajamas with feet, in the middle of winter as the Old Man drove away.

Brett never said a word. He just quietly whimpered as I had my arm around him. We stood there for a moment just trying to process what was going on. I looked both ways trying to recognize something. I had no idea where we were so I tried to review in my head the turns we had taken and the glimpses of things I saw along the way. We slowly walked down the cold dark streets as I attempted to guide us back to Grandma's house. There were no bread crumbs, and there was definitely no kind Huntsman who rode in to rescue us. Just Brett and I freezing our butts off trying to figure out which way to go.

After a couple wrong turns and a few doublings back I started to recognize some landmarks. Our pace quickened as I started to realize that I just might be able to get us back before our feet froze. As we made the last turn, I could see my mom huddled on the front steps.

"Ma!" I yelled.

She looked up and ran to us bawling.

"Oh, my God," she gasped, grabbing us both at the same time. She squeezed real hard.

"I can't believe you made it."

She rushed us inside to warm up. She rubbed our feet and hands while she exclaimed how brave we were and how smart I was to figure out how to get back. She got us into warm dry clothes, put us in the boots I wish I had had earlier and drove us home.

As we drove back home in the middle of the night and my mom continued to brag about how brave and smart I was to get us back, I felt a swell of pride. In a twisted way I felt like I had beat the Old Man. He left us there in order to hurt my mom, not caring about what happened to Brett and me, but I got us back. It was a little victory, I know, but in a world when I could not battle the Old Man physically, and I could not even stand up to him verbally, this time on the dark cold streets of who-knows-where I beat him. I beat him while wearing my pajamas.

BRETT
Hampton

We took a long drive to Hampton Beach in New Hampshire every summer where the beach was packed with people. Blankets covered the sand with inches between them for as far as the eye could see. The colors would shimmer in the August heat. Adults slathered with oil and cooked in the sun as their kids played in the icy cold Atlantic. Brady and I would come out of the water shivering, lips blue, and with big smiles on our faces. The sand was so hot we had to tip-toe with yelps in between each step. We would run up to the tiny island of towels our family had staked out for the day to get a snack or to try and get Uncle Phil to peel himself off the blanket and come and race us.

"Come on Uncle Phil!"

"You guys aren't fast enough," he would mutter without raising his head.

I knew he was smiling under those taunting words.

"You said you would race us in a few minutes, and it has been more than a few minutes!" I always pleaded.

"Are you two going to make me get up just to have to walk all the way down there and beat you?" he would say with his sinister smile. Uncle Phil loved to pretend that our requests were the biggest inconvenience in the world. He would let out this huge exaggerated yawn and then sneer.

"Go make the starting line."

The word "line" wasn't even out of his mouth, and Brady and I would already be racing toward the water to carve the start and finish line in the hard-packed sand the high tide waters had left behind. Brady and I would jump up and down and sprint around bragging about how much we had been practicing on our "speed."

"Oh, really?" He pretended to be disinterested, as if our progress did not concern him in the least. His fake apathy purposely built up the anticipation that we would both have for our races. He would make it close, but he never let us win. Uncle Phil would grant us a handful of races where he would act tired and pretend to exert maximum effort in trying to keep us from winning. However, it didn't take a mastermind to understand he was taking it easy on my brother and me. Brady and I would try everything. We would jump the start signal, we would try to grab our Uncle's arms, or try and trip him -- to no avail. The fact that he never let us win, as he well knew, is why we always came back to beg for more races summer after summer.

Every season our family would chip in and get a cottage for a few weeks at Hampton Beach. It was a time I never wanted to end. My Mom, Auntie Ju, and Uncle Phil all overlapped their weeks in order to allow us to have the property for a longer period of time, and my brother, Mimi and I got to stay the whole time. I heard the 'adult talks' each spring of how they would scrape the funds together to get a cottage each summer. It was not an easy task finding a place and paying for it even with everyone chipping in, but this time was precious for everyone, so even in the extremely lean years they somehow made it work.

We would spend the days flying kites, building sand castles, and body surfing in the Atlantic waves. When the sun went down we would cover our sun-baked skin with light sweatshirts in order to protect against the ocean breeze and head out for our "evening excursion." Our family would meander along the boardwalk looking into shops, getting ice cream and playing mini golf. I would hold on to Mimi's hand confessing dreams of one day being this or having that.

At sixty, Mimi was the the eldest in our family, but she was still the biggest dreamer. She would still say, "when I grow up I want to be…" My mother would chuckle about how many 'dreamers' we had in the family. The verdict was still out whether wishful thinking was a good thing or a bad thing. So many of us embraced these future plans of owning something, going somewhere, doing something with such passion, but there was always an undercurrent of disbelief. We never confirmed if the current state of our existence weighed so heavy that it didn't allow us to fully believe in our better future. So we called them our dreams.

As we traveled north along the boardwalk the mansions became visible along the cliffs overlooking the ocean. We would always talk about chipping in and buying one of them so we could live on the beach year around. The idea of all of us being together in one big mansion overlooking the ocean and taking these walks everyday was what I longed for as a young kid. We decided that we would call our mansion on the hill Moon Point.

Mimi always made those wind-swept dreams seem possible. She would whisper in my ear, and the drama of Seven Grove Street would get pulled out with the tide. Those strong waves would pound at the aches and pains of my regular life as Mimi's soft voice would cut the last stubborn nightmare free, and the ocean would wash all my anxiety away. The hot sand, the carnival sounds, and Mimi's soft hands would take over. So as we walked she put her arms around me and confided stories of ancient Indians and fearless warriors from the books that she read. My ears belonged to her, and these secrets were ours.

"Brett you can do whatever you want if you put your mind to it."

"Brett you are such a good boy, just keep making Mimi proud."

When I described to her the good deeds I did in school that year like helping the teacher clean the board or clapping the dusty erasers outside she would say, "That makes Mimi's heart sing."

Lacing her stories of warriors and dreams were little positive things she would say to me about how good I was and how much she loved me. Her recognition made me want to make her proud. I would fight with myself to stay positive and try not to get into mischief during the school year because of those walks.

Night after night I would find Mimi's arm and listen to her stories as people bustled by and lights flashed. Our group would string out along the the boardwalk, casually searching the pizza joint we might have decided to go to that night. But Mimi and I had our own pace, and there was simply no other place on the planet I wanted to be during that time.

Hampton Beach was like the dreams we constructed on our evening walks. The summer heat, lights, and sounds were always replaced by the winter silence. Hampton Beach was a ghost town in the winter. The pizza joints, arcades, and shops were boarded up for the season; only the pounding of the surf remained. Each one of my passionate fantasies seemed to be elusive. During the summer glow the picture was right at my fingertips -- living and breathing and with Mimi's voice -- so real. However, when the cool fall winds slowly turned the beach to winter and the boards were nailed up to protect the glass from the February storms, the images would get blacked out too. Warm vibrant pictures were replaced by cold dark silence and the desolate beach.

BRADY
The Shark

When my brother and I were really young, my instinct was to flee. His instinct was to fight. As far back as I can remember he would run towards potential confrontation while I would run away. I remember being on the playground in elementary school playing dodgeball, and I caught the ball that Mike Mahoney threw. He didn't go out of the game. As every kid knows you are supposed to go out of the game when someone catches your throw.

"You're out," I said.

"No I am not. You have something to say about it?" he replied.

I must have looked stupid because it took me a bit of time to wrap my mind around the part Mike wasn't getting. In my mind it was simple: I caught the ball and his dumb ass was out. However, Mike figured that because he was so much bigger than me, that the rules of dodgeball (which I thought that all of humanity agreed upon) did not apply to him.

He walked right up to me and started pushing. I was in shock. Everyone watching said that he was out. Even Duncan said it, and

34

he was playing with bugs by the stonewall with a finger up his nose. I mean, come on, if you have a guy with a finger up his nose weighing in then you know it must be true.

"Nichols, you have a problem?" Mike was saying as he kept shoving me.

Thoughts started flooding my brain as to what to do: push him back, turn and run, punch him in the face, start to cry? Picture after picture kept flashing in my head. As Mike shoved me a couple more times, I stood there like a moron.

My brother, who was smaller than me, was across the school yard playing basketball. He noticed what was occurring from across the whole asphalt playground. When the tussle took a step further, from shoving to a headlock, Brett ran over and jumped on Mike's back.

"Get the hell off my brother!" he screamed.

Brett didn't know what our altercation was about, and he didn't care. He was in the middle of a game of his own and just sprinted across the playground to get at him. Mike was twice our size. Brett didn't care. He was always reckless and I was always cautious. If we were doing jumps with our bikes behind the old shop after school, he would always have to make his jumps bigger. He would always come at things faster than anyone else. He would always make things higher than anyone else.

There were a couple great climbing trees by the river near our house, and he would go to the very top of them. I would be lucky to get halfway. The wind would make the tops sway like crazy. The branches grew so thin past the halfway point that I would ask him if he was ever scared that the branches wouldn't hold him.

"Aww, they aren't going to break. If they do there are other branches right below them to grab onto," he would say with a grin.

After our little scuffle in the school yard was broken up by a couple teachers, all three of us got sent to the principal's office. Walking home from school, I yelled at Brett for getting into trouble over my altercation.

"I was helping you out." He used the tone that was saying, "I can't believe you are getting on me right now because I was sticking up for you."

"I can take care of myself Brett. I don't need you jumping in and getting into trouble too," I shot back. From as early as I can remember, my first instinct was to do whatever I could to keep Brett out of trouble.

Mom grounded my brother over that incident and didn't ground me. She punished him because 'he fought too much.' I wouldn't get into trouble for the playground incident because my mother, for whatever instinctual reason, just knew that I didn't start anything. Perhaps she knew that I was just a big chicken too. It didn't matter. Brett would get grounded for fighting because he always fought.

To tell you the truth, he really didn't jump on Mike Mahoney's back that day to help me out. Yeah, part of it was that, but the real reason was that it was an excuse. My brother just found any reason to fight. He loved confrontation. He had no problem getting hit, and he sure as heck had no problem hitting back. Most of the time, from what I saw, he gave a whole lot more than he took. There was something dark in his eyes that most people didn't have, like dark eyes of the shark patrolling the seas having absolutely no fear. That darkness made me recognize quite early that my brother was ready to go to a place that others weren't willing to go: throw more punches, climb higher, fall further. I only knew one other person who had that darkness in his eyes, and that was the Old Man.

BRETT
Manhole Cover

O ne day we decided to get some bait for fishing. We planned
on heading to the Three Pipes, the official site of our favorite fishing spot. It was called Three Pipes simply because there
were three large pipes there. On one side of an old dirt road was a
lake and on other side was a river. The three pipes joined the two.
Water rushed through the three pipes and we climbed all around
the area looking for the best spot to catch fish. Trout was on the
river side, and pickerel was on the lake side. We were pumped to
jump on our bikes and get there as soon as possible.

We needed bait, so with our shovel in hand, a group of us set
out towards The Shop. The Shop was the old furniture factory behind our house. The place seemed abandoned half the time, and
we crawled all over it inside and out when no one was around. We
jumped off the roof and crept around inside. There was this one
patch of field by The Shop where we would dig for worms. We dug
and dug but got nothing. We, however did find a manhole cover:
one of those big heavy iron disks that cover up a hole in the middle

of the street. This one was sitting in the middle of this field probably having something to do with The Shop.

Being one of the youngest and most naive kids in the group, I thought there might actually be some worms under the cover.

"Let's get under this thing and see what is underneath."

"Dumb idea," the others said. "These things are heavy as hell."

I really thought there was an endless supply of worms underneath, so I convinced everyone to just one look. We wedged the tip of the shovel in the crack between the manhole and the ledge it rested on. With everyone leaning hard on our shovel handle, we got it to move.

"We can lift this thing," I said, "but only if we all get our hands under and lift at the same time."

Some of the guys started to lose interest and walked away.

"That thing is too heavy man, let's go."

I was determined. I was certain that if I lifted this plate up, we would strike gold. After most of the crew walked away, I became even more focused on proving them all wrong. I got a nice firm grip with both hands on the cover. As I tried to lift the iron plate, the shovel slipped out.

As soon as that shovel slipped, I realized how heavy that manhole cover really was. I felt the true weight of the cover. The shovel created the space for my hands to feel like they were lifting, and not my brute strength. It was at that moment it occurred to me that maybe I wasn't that strong. It was at that moment that I knew I was screwed.

I tried to pull my hands out before the cover crashed down on my fingers. All I could do was scream. Brady came running over and wedged the shovel back into the crack and raised it just enough for me to pull my fingers out. Most of the kids were frozen in their steps just staring.

I couldn't feel my hand as I pulled it free. My middle finger was mangled. When I saw the gnarled mess that once looked like a finger, I started to scream. Brady tore up the street yelling for my mom to get the car started.

"I am going to die!" I cried as I stumbled up the street towards our house. Blood was all over my shirt, and I was a mess. It didn't take Mom long to recognize that this was a crisis situation. My mother worked in the emergency room at the local hospital, and she was certainly a woman of action. You spilled something on the counter and the second it hit the surface she had it wiped up. She did nothing slow. She walked fast, talked fast, and in moments like this, she reacted fast. She stepped out on the stoop to see me and Brady screaming and yelling. In a flash she was out of the house with car keys in hand.

As I moaned in the car, my mother kept telling me to calm down. I was convinced I was going to die. I was in the front seat demanding that the window be down so I could breathe. My feet stretched and writhed out the window. I wasn't even capable of relishing the fact that I got to sit in the front seat for once. By the time we got to the hospital, my mom had calmed me to the point of believing that I had a chance to live.

About the time I started to calm down, the doctor came into the emergency room and had a conversation with my mom using a bunch of terms I didn't understand. I started to worry all over again that maybe those terms were hinting to the fact that my life was now turning for the worse again. It was turning for the worse all right. It turned for the worse once he started cleaning the wound. The alcohol or whatever he used to clean my deformed finger burned like it was engulfed in flames and my screaming started up all over again. This time my pain was mixed with anger at this doctor for creating all the agony again. I begged him to stop. He told me that it would just take a minute and we had to clean this wound. My begging turned to threats.

"If you don't stop I am going to call my dad to beat you up."

I assumed everyone knew my dad. We had so many instances where people warned my mom about what he was doing around town that it seemed only logical that this guy would know of him.

"Seriously, if you don't stop my dad is going to come here and kick your ass!" I screamed.

I also figured everyone was as afraid of my father as I was. I promised this proper looking guy in a white lab coat that if he touched me again he was going to regret it.

As we finally left, I stared at my hand and how it was now in a splint with stitches raw and rough poking through. I started to feel like a big deal. I never had stitches before. I had been through a battle and was feeling tough and somewhat validated.

We never got to the Three Pipes that day. Shoot, we never even found a worm that day. Like so many other things, our trophy fish was just out of reach, mocking us. My trophy instead was a messed up hand.

BRADY
Knuckle Marks

The Old Man had a drinking problem. Much of our early childhood consisted of my Mom working her ass off to raise my brother and me. The Old Man was gone most of the time, and when he was home, he was drunk and busting up the house or smacking my mom around. It was not uncommon for my brother and me to be playing and my mom rushing into the room out of the blue to scoop us up and throw us in the car to drive to Mimi's house because Ma got some call from a friend that our father was coming home from the bar drunk and enraged. As a young kid it felt as if we were always on edge. It seemed as soon as the three of us started to relax, he would come crashing back to bring his angry mayhem.

My mom's vulnerable moments seemed to happen in our bathroom on Grove Street. Locked behind the door with a cigarette and sitting on the edge of the tub is where I would find her when things got tough. If I knocked real soft she would let me in and I would sit by her feet. The veiled responses were always:

"Nothing Brady don't worry."

"I am all right your father just scared me - that is all"

"I am just tired from work."

None of these answers made me feel better. They didn't make me feel safe or more calm. And even as a little kid I knew she was not telling me what was really going on. Instead, I felt small and angry. He would smack us around and bust stuff up and there was nothing that I could do. It took all that I had to not piss myself when he went into one of his rages.

So often before he had plowed through the front door late at night when Brett and I were sleeping. We heard him pounding on the door. Yelling. We heard the soft voice of my mother trying to hush him not to wake us. We heard the muffled arguing and the shattering of glass. Whimpering. My mother's footsteps coming closer. She slammed the door to her bedroom that was across from the basement room my brother and I shared. His heavy footsteps were coming closer, and now I was wide awake and getting more worried by the second. The longer these events lasted the worse they always turned out. The Old Man first started gently to ask my mother to open the door in a fake tone. She didn't. He then demanded that she open the door. She didn't. He then started to pound on the door. This created so much noise in the middle of the night I hoped that someone next door would hear and come and call the police. No one did. The pounding turned into a couple of sharp cracks. Soon after his feet retreated back upstairs so he could start more destruction. As he started to smash crap upstairs, I would try to envision what he was breaking based on where he stood upstairs. I wished I had X Ray vision so I could get a sense of where he was. There was always a level of comfort from knowing he was in another room wreaking havoc because it meant he was further away from me.

He finally left the house, and we heard the Nova peeling off in the distance. My mother, brother and I laid still for a bit in the silence to make sure the storm had passed. My brother and I went to my mother's room and noticed that the door had a deep series of knuckle marks on it. That feeling of being the smallest creature on the planet came back. His massive fist created this huge gash in the door. The one thing that stood between him and my mother was the stupid door, and I could do nothing but hide under the covers and hope he would go away, and hope even more that those fists didn't turn my way. I was flooded with anger for being so small, so skinny, so useless. I remembered weeks ago when my mother was talking to a friend about her crooked nose that was busted by her new husband's fist when I was just a baby. My mother was one of the most beautiful women in the world in my young eyes. After I overheard that story, I would study Ma's face and search for the faint bump on the bridge of her nose. This horrible imperfection for her was quite different for me. Nothing would diminish her beauty in my eyes.

In the morning we would walk up stairs to see the upper level rearranged by his anger. Furniture would be knocked over and busted. Most glassware would be shattered against walls or broken on the floor. I will never forget my mom particularly upset about the cookie jar. The cookie jar remained unbroken. So many things in the kitchen were destroyed, but the cookie jar just sat there un-harmed. And it was this object my mother went straight to.

"Damn." She let out as she looked inside.

A moment of confusion filled me. I thought, "Cookies, now mom? Our house looks like a tornado hit it. Most of our belong-ings are destroyed, and you are upset because there are no cookies in the cookie jar. Shoot, I could tell you there haven't been cookies in the cookie jar for months. Plus, you should know because you bake the darn cookies anyway."

Instead I paused and looked up as tears started to stream down her face.

Hugging her leg I looked up and asked her what was wrong.

"He stole the money I stashed in the jar. I had hidden the money in the cookie jar."

She then just broke down on the kitchen floor and my brother and I sat on either side of her.

The complexity of this attack started to weigh on me. For the man that was our father would not only physically hurt our family, he would not only destroy the objects in our home, but he would then systematically take the money that my mother worked for. It created a new sort of loathing for me as I started to understand this battle that my mother continued to fight. It always seemed like a losing battle in my younger days.

Regardless, many of these events ended with a period of calm or worse a period of promise where the Old Man would come back swearing that he had changed and things would be different. My mother might have had some hope, but I never did. Sometimes these periods almost got to normal but only for a short while. They never were long enough to melt away the bone-chilling tension that I always felt in this man's presence. I would overhear the adults saying it was like 'walking on eggshells' around my father. No one ever knew when his temper would flare. 'Eggshells' I thought? I would much rather walk on eggshells. For me it was like walking on broken glass with no shoes when he was around. Watch where you step because if you step wrong, you are going to be in some pain.

BRETT
Green Hornet

It was a beautiful Saturday morning, and I had just pounded about five bowls of cereal. When Brady and I agreed to help my Mom grocery shop, she let us pick out some 'sugar' cereal. That meant that instead of muscling down Total or oatmeal, we got Lucky Charms or Apple Jacks. I could easily eat five bowls of sugar cereal like it was nothing.

I was about to bolt out the door to play when my father called me over. I could smell the beer leaking out of his pores.

"Where are you going?" he asked without even opening his eyes.

"Can we go out and play?" I asked.

He opened one eye to say, "Don't go far. If I call, you better be able to hear me."

He loaned a watch and reminded us to be back by 4pm. This was big time because Brady didn't get the instructions; for once I did. I tightened the watch on my wrist, and Brady and I met the crew outside. They had been waiting.

We decided to head down to the 'Quarter Mile," a stretch of abandoned road that had concrete barriers so vehicles couldn't get down it unless they went off road somehow. The high school kids loved to go to the end of the road and party, and we loved to go to the end of the road to see what they left behind the following morning. Dirt bike trails went off into the woods on all sides of this quarter mile stretch of road. We had explored every inch back there growing up. Popping wheelies on our bikes and getting excited at what would be left behind from the previous Friday night was always an adventure. At the end of the Quarter Mile was a stream, and Highway 202 passed high above. When we arrived, we dropped our bikes and saw that there was a smoldering campfire.

For the first few minutes, we all went off in separate directions to see what we could find. There were charred sticks, bottles, rubbish, and tire marks everywhere. Not much else was around except for smoldering coals. Surprisingly, some of the logs were still glowing red. We chastised the high school kids for leaving such a fire hazard, and then immediately started to stomp on the glowing embers. Bored, we soon turned to throwing old charred logs into the center to watch the explosion of sparks. Some of the guys threw bottles into the pit. The sparks would kick out like fireworks floating into the air.

It quickly became a contest to see who could produce the most sparks from launching random debris into the glowing embers. There was an absence of time as we cheered and prodded one another along. As our antics came to an end and we got tired of the game, we were covered in soot and charcoal. Glancing at my watch, I noticed that it read a few minutes after 2pm. As we all studied each other, we began to crack up. We were blanketed by black soot, and we didn't really notice how filthy we were until we looked at the other guy.

When we decided to go, we lazily walked our bikes down the road and talked about the 'fireworks' we created. That came to a halt just as I glanced at my watch and realized that it still read a bit after 2pm. That is when I realized that my watch had stopped. My heart jumped right into my throat. "What time is it?"

Then Brian said as he looked down the road, "Is that your Dad?"

The 'Green Hornet' was the name we gave my Dad's Chevy Nova. Seeing the 'Green Hornet' prowling down the road, where cars were not allowed to drive, and making out my Dad's tattooed arm hanging out the open driver's side window, almost made my heart stop as my watch had. Reality dropped straight down on my skull. The watch Dad loaned me had stopped working hours ago, he had been calling, we obviously never heard him, and now he was fuming. The arm resting on the open window raised up and pointed at us - forearm fully flexed and index finger straight as a dart. It pointed at us in a manner that clearly said, "I'm boiling mad and you two are in big trouble." It felt as if his pointed finger hit me right between the eyes.

When we reached the car the rest of the crew just kept walking with their heads down. They did not utter a word.

He stepped out of the Hornet and his face alone told us everything we needed to know. This was going to be really bad for us. He silently he opened the trunk, grabbed our bikes with each arm, and slammed them into the trunk. He threw them in as if his intent was to make them break.

As we stood motionless with him looking down at us, fear gripped me so hard that I literally wet myself. He opened the back door of the Hornet and grabbed us, one hand gripping an arm and the other the back of our pants as he threw us into the back of the car like we were sacks of flour.

He got into the driver's seat. Not one word was spoken until all doors were closed and the windows were rolled up. He used the rear view mirror to make eye contact.

"I have been calling you two for an hour!"

"What happened to the damn watch Brett!"

He screamed and carried on about how useless we were and that he had to waste his time to come find us.

When we got home we got our butts beat. He threw us around the house as we put our bikes away, smacked us around and yelled as we went into the bathroom to clean up, and kept at it until we went to our room. As he followed us the more agitated he became. Brady and I never said a word. We knew it was pointless to explain anything. It made sense to just take it. Ride it out and hope that it would end as painlessly and quickly as possible.

It wasn't the worst whooping that we ever got. Not even close. However, from that day forward, just the sight of the Hornet created a stinging anxiety. As we grew up, the prowling Green Hornet would stalk my mother and us around town, always lurking and reminding us that we might never be free.

BRADY
Egg Fight

Mimi had taught us many ways to get the colors to swirl. It was always fun to try and see which colors looked the best together. Brett and I would always turn everything into a competition. Who would have the best egg? Which effect looked the coolest? Some years for Easter Mimi would have us blow the yolk out so we would paint the hollow egg. I hated when we did that because our cheeks would kill after blowing that thick yolk out of those tiny holes. Our heads felt like they were going to explode. Mimi always had the best eggs in the end; her colors and effects were always so much better than my brother's and mine. When I was in fifth grade we hardboiled the eggs and painted them afterward. Mimi told us we could not keep the eggs as long because we hardboiled them. They would start to rot after a week, she told us. We didn't care, as long as we didn't have to blow yolk out of those tiny holes and make every vein in our heads feel like it was going to pop.

A week or so after Easter, Mom threatened to chuck the eggs out because she said they would stink up the house. So before she had the chance to collect our stockpile and throw them in the garbage, Brett and I grabbed the decorated orbs and went outside. We laid the dozen or so on the ground and evened them out between us. In our front yard, standing apart from one another, we eyed each other down. We were two gunslingers waiting to see who would twitch first. Projectiles in hand, we grinned waiting for the other to make a move. I went with the full-on assault. I threw mine in a rapid fire sequence, as Brett dove from side to side trying not to get hit. Unfortunately, I didn't really get any direct hits; they were all just glancing blows. To add insult to injury, he had yet to fire one. I had no eggs left, and he had all of his.

Brett was probably in third grade at the time. Being the older brother by 18 months, I would try to pull rank on him every so often. If we were getting in the car with Mom to go somewhere, I would be like, "Man, I am the oldest - out of the front seat!" Often a fight resulted so my Mom instituted some mechanism that included alternating. Her strategy worked for pretty much everything: pushing the cart at the grocery store, the last bowl of cereal, or nearly every toy we played with. Pulling rank on my little brother was like an inheritance; as far as I was concerned, it was probably written somewhere in the Constitution: *Thou gets first dibs by virtue of being first born.* Even though there isn't a proclamation stating that, certainly there should have been.

As Brett as stood there with all his eggs and with a big grin while my hands were empty, it seemed like the perfect time to put the Big Brother Clause into effect.

"Brett, you hit me with one of those eggs and you are a dead man!"

"That is bull crap. You threw all yours," he shouted. "I get to throw all mine."

"You do and you will pay!"

Well, I knew the warning was a futile effort. My warning had no effect. He launched his eggs one after the other. I dodged and

weaved as he did. Things were going great. He wasn't getting any
real hits--until the last one, of course. The final freaking egg, as I
spun around, nailed me right in the middle of the back. Just then
I remembered that Brett made the Little League team and I didn't.
He had a great arm. That last beautifully painted, hard boiled
egg, crunched me right square between the shoulder blades.

"Damn!"

I fell to one knee. Brett froze. This was the kind of moment
that was so crucial to all our battles. The next few minutes dic-
tated the end game: peace or more war. My brother waited as he
watched me kneeling with my back turned to him. Some days
he'd hear a "nice shot man," whether it be a basketball or a punch.
Some days it was " I am going to kill you," whether it be basketball
or a punch. Today it was latter. He took off in a full sprint toward
the back of the house. I rose and darted to just a few steps behind.

Chasing my brother was probably one of the pleasurable things
I ever did in my childhood. I was older and faster. Sometimes I
gave him head starts like the one he had right now. Depending on
the circumstances, he would run at full speed either giggling or
crying. For his first few strides I think he believed that he would
actually get away. Then, as the little dance we so often performed
wore on, it was clear I was gaining on him. He jumped old stumps,
ran around yard furniture and even threw items, but in the end he
knew that I was going to catch him.

This time I didn't catch him. As Brett ripped around the corner,
cutting it too sharp in order to gain an advantage on me, he smashed
his face on the table of the old bandsaw my father had leaning
against the house. Brett had taken a peek back to see if I was gaining as he rounded the corner, and when he turned around, WHAM!
His chin smacked right into the protruding metal platform. The
collision cut his legs out right from underneath him. As he hit the
ground, my whole intent changed instantly. I went from search-
and-destroy mode to holy-crap-my-brother-just-smashed-his-face

mode. I ran over to him and saw that his chin was gashed open pretty wide. He was crying. The egg fight, revenge, anger, and chase was finished. All that melted away. It was now my little brother hurt, and he needed me.

I helped him put pressure on the cut, and we went bloodied and bruised to our Mom who first made sure it wasn't a life or death situation. Then she gave us the business: "You two never learn!" she said. She took Brett to the hospital to get a couple stitches, and let us just say I learned an important lesson that day: never hurl all your eggs at once and save a couple for the end game.

BRETT
Jack

Behind our house was the old chair factory. In front of our house was Highway 202. When we were little, the crew and I would head up the dirt hill to play in a small field next to the highway. On the other side of the streaming traffic were 'nice houses.' We would sometimes go across and hang around. Sometimes we even visited people we knew over on that side. Most of the time, however, we remained in our little world on our side of the highway. The grassy patch had tall grass where we could hide out and create games while traffic zoomed by. My brother and the older kids would always come up with something.

Sometimes we caught grasshoppers and brought them home. Other times we divided into teams and had milkweed pod wars. Occassionaly we got bored and threw them at passing trucks. We dove into the tall grass to hide. If we ever saw brake lights after a direct hit we dashed the opposite way into the woods. We tried to get far away, worried that the driver might come and find us. Many lazy afternoons were spent up there just filling the time with whatever entered our minds.

One day we were hanging out at the field when I saw my cat, Jack. He was my pride and joy. I had rescued him the previous year near my 4th grade school. When I found him, he was skinny with patches of fur missing and seemed barely alive. I would sneak him milk behind the dumpsters at recess every day and we bonded. He began to put on weight and looked healthier. I talked my mom into letting me take him home, which wasn't easy because my brother is allergic to fur. She let me keep him around as an outdoor cat. She was more concerned about my ability to commit to taking care of him.

"Brett, you have the tendency to start stuff and not follow through," she lectured.

I told my mom I could totally take care of the cat and was doing a good job so far too. I fed him every day, and he adored me. Jack loved to chill on my lap, purring away. He would prowl around the neighborhood, but always came back to our house to get fed. Jack was a bruiser. When he gained his weight back, he was a monster of a cat and all we saw him do was hunt. He even had these double paws that had extra toes. Being nine going on ten, all us guys valued being tough, and we saw Jack as one tough cat.

So as we ran around the field that summer day, Jack was hunting mice as usual. We saw him pounce on dozens of field mice up there. When he heard us playing in the field, he rushed right over to me. Having this sleek creature come over to me by its own free will felt so empowering. Just as he sat purring in my arms, I saw a black cat cross the highway over to our neighborhood. As everyone pet Jack, impressed by my loyal and fierce pet, the house cat with a red collar did not even look in our direction. I decided I wanted to show Jack off more.

"Hey, let's call that cat over and see if he and Jack will fight," I suggested.

"I don't know, Brett. That cat seems wimpy. Jack would probably maul it." Ben said in protest.

Soon I convinced them that it was worth it, and we called the small black cat over.

"Here kitty, kitty," I said in my sweetest voice.

As the cat turned our way and nearly reached us, I threw Jack toward the unsuspecting prey. Jack reared up and pounced on it. He batted the black cat around a couple times. They hissed at each other, and the black cat bolted for home. Home for this cat was across the highway. As the cat sprinted full speed across the road, a big truck flattened him instantly without a notice. We all screamed. A couple of the guys even fell to their knees in disbelief.

"Brett, what the hell man! Look what you did."

"Aww. No man." Ben groaned.

"What did you do?"

"I'm sorry. I didn't know it would get hit!" I tried to defend myself.

Jack went about his business without hesitation and just meandered toward the tree line as if nothing happened. Meanwhile, we all ran over to the highway and waited for a break in the traffic. As we stood over the body, I felt sick. In trying to prove my toughness through Jack, I clearly went too far.

"This is messed up," Brady said.

As we stood on the side of the road, we debated what to do.

"We can't leave it there."

"We have to find the owner and let them know that their cat is dead at least."

As the guys continued to lay a guilt trip on me, we headed back to the house to get a shovel and bag. We decided that we had to bury it, but first had to let the owner know. We came back to the site, and between breaks in traffic, we scraped the corpse off the asphalt and into a trash bag. We then headed for the nice side of the highway. We knocked on doors asking people if they owned a cat. If they said 'yes,' we asked them if it was black.

After a handful of houses said no, we reached a tidy little house. After ringing the doorbell, an old lady came to the door.

"Hello. Do you own a cat?"

"Yes," the frail old lady replied. We began to shrink in shame.

"Is, is it black?" we asked.

"Yes," she responded. Kevin, one of the littlest guys in our crew, started to cry knowing what was about to come next.

We showed her the little red collar.

"Is this the collar?"

She confirmed the collar was her cat's, and we told her that it got hit by a truck. Not brave enough to expose our roles in the cat's demise, we left out the fact that it ran because my dumb ass tried to make it fight. She was visibly very upset. She quivered a bit, and her eyes got red, and then she thanked us for being so kind as to let her know. She thanked us. She actually thanked us. Guilt... horrible guilt set in as we all slumped away.

We told her that we would bury the cat for her in a pet cemetery that a guy down the road created.

"Oh, thank you boys. You are all so kind."

From the time she said, "thank you," to the actual burial, we even made a headstone, but none of us said a word. We didn't grunt or whisper a thing. We just went through motions and hoped that our funeral would make it right because we all felt so wrong.

About a month later, we stood in Old Man Johnny's pet cemetery in complete silence and dug a hole. This time the hole was for Jack. A couple weeks back Jack stopped coming around, and I noticed he wasn't eating the food I was leaving out. I spent days looking for him. The crew helped. We gave up after a week. Then, sure enough, the next time we went to play in the highway field, we noticed him dead on the side of the road.

"You think this is Karma?" Ben asked.

"Shut the hell up man," I demanded. But inside I still felt wrong. Karma. Yeah, maybe Ben was right.

BRADY
Checkers

"Keep it down dammit!"

The Old Man laid on the couch half watching tv and half trying to sleep off the night before. Being stuck in the house with him was brutal. The rain outside did not stop. It banged on the roof all morning long. He could not tolerate loud noises when he was hungover, and he was hungover a lot. When our mother worked, and we were stuck at home with him, we just tried to stay out of his way as much as possible.

On this morning my brother and I played checkers in the room next to him. Half way through the game, my brother made a silly face and I started laughing. He did stuff like that to me. We may have fought a lot, argued and pummeled each other at times, but on the other hand, the kid made me laugh like no other. It stunk when someone made me laugh and I was not supposed to, like in church or class. It was like the more inappropriate the harder it was to stop. It turned into an uncontrollable laughter. I hated that. I despised it even more when I knew that our laughter was going to send my half-drunk father into a rage.

When my brother saw me painfully trying to hold it in, he started to giggle. It was a hand-over-mouth-holding-most-of-it-in type of laugh at first. However, it unfortunately slipped out of control into a laughing-out-loud-pretty-hard-laugh.

"God Dammit. Shut the hell up. Don't make me come in there!" the Old Man growled.

This was not good. I whispered to Brett that we should take the game downstairs where the Old Man could not hear every little thing. Good idea. Smart. We did not want him flipping out, so it was probably best to get far away. I always came up with practical ideas like that. Sometimes the ideas worked, and sometimes they didn't. Unfortunately this time my scheme didn't. When my brother stood up, the tablecloth got caught on his belt buckle. He dragged everything with him by accident: he moved it a little, not a ton, but enough. The checkerboard was sitting on the table cloth, and when he took a step from the table, the checkers and the board crashed to the floor.

"You two just don't get it, do you?"

Our father jumped off of the couch immediately, like he had been just waiting all day to pounce. All morning he slouched around half dead asking me to get him this and that. He was on the couch for hours as if his legs were broken. But now, when the checkers hit the floor, he sprang into a screaming, shouting and snarling fit. My brother and I had been batted around by the Old Man way too many times to count, so when we heard him scrambling like that, we had one thing in mind: move away fast.

I loved watching *Animal Kingdom* at Mimi's house and I remember learning about the wildebeest of Africa. Animals have flight or fight instincts. Some animals, like lions, are aggressors, and it is in their nature to fight to survive. On the crappy side of the coin there are animals that have to be skittish to survive, like wildebeests. When the Old Man charged like that, it meant that he was ready for a fight. It meant we had to get the hell out of the way. For us it meant to flee like the wildebeest.

When he cornered us in the room, I backed up putting the table between the two of us. My brother was next to me.

"Get over here. Get over here now!"

He edged slowly towards us. He moved to his right. We walked the other way, keeping the separation.

"So help me God, you better get your ass over here now!"

This side-to-side dance went on for only a few minutes, but it seemed like hours. Each minute of this waltz made him angrier. His blood was at full boil. I imagined his rage making the same sizzling sound that water makes when it hits a hot pan on the stove. The Old Man's fury was boiling over, about to rip off our roof and flood the streets. He finally committed to a direction and went full speed to the left. My brother and I countered by sprinting all out to our left. As I rounded the corner, the front door was only one room away. I had nothing in mind except the exit, to get it open and run as far down the Seven Grove Street as I could.

We dashed for the door as he continued to cuss and grunt. I heard a faint monologue of what he was going to do to us when he caught us. All I cared about was getting to the great wet and miserable outdoors. I just wanted to hit the front yard and keep running.

My brother was two grades below me. I tried, in my older brotherly way, to keep him with me, but as the table dance with the Old Man ended we had to sprint for our lives like the wildebeest. I bolted out the front door and down the yard. As Brett was about to jump off the stoop, he was caught in the jaws of the lion. I ran down the road crying. I hated myself. I wanted to turn and fight. I wanted to face the Old Man and make him leave my brother alone. Unfortunately, the hunted do not think like that; sometimes regardless of whom they leave behind they just run.

BRETT
The Pickle

O n the way to Three Pipes was the old ball field behind the
Shop. That was where we played football and baseball when
we gathered enough of the crew together. It was where I acquired
the skills that helped me make the Little League team the first
year I tried out. I knew that making it the first year was something
to be proud of because Brady had tried out the first year he was
old enough and didn't make it.

I was placed on the Red Sox. It was the first real team that I
was ever on. Baseball was my first love. I listened to whatever the
coach told me and then went home to practice. I bounced the
ball against the side of the Shop for hours. I went back to the field
and caught pop flies with Ben and Kevin many afternoons. When
Brady and our crew went together to the ball field, we loved to play
Pickle. We placed one guy on second, another on third, and then
we rotated runners in an attempt to beat them. The second and
third basemen leisurely threw the ball back and forth, purposely making mistakes in order to entice a runner to bolt for third.

When the runner was off the bag, the 'pickle' started. When the defense threw the ball back and forth, it slowly squeezed the runner. Every player laughed the whole time, enjoying the anticipation of that breaking point when the runner would get tagged out, or slip by the defense making it safely to third.

Those pickle games got me prepared for my days in Little League. My Red Sox team played most of our games in Phillipston, a town nearby, where the field had concessions and plenty of parking for the spectators. Cars parked right up to the fence and honked horns when someone made a nice hit. The carnival feel made the players feel important; it made them want to have a good game. Our coach got all fired up. I loved listening to his pump-us-up-speeches and absorbed all the tips he gave us: keep your eye on the ball, step into your swing, and elbows up before swinging the bat. It felt like he was telling us secrets that other kids didn't know. He spent every practice trying to make us better, and all I wanted was to be better.

My brother and my mother came to all of the games. Mimi didn't have her driver's license so she was not able to come often to cheer for me. My Mom had to go way out of the way to get her and bring her back home. So when Mimi came to watch, that made the game extra special to me. The game against the Tigers ended up being a close one. It was stopped for a moment because Seb, one of Brady's friends, got struck in the eye by a wild pitch. He dropped hard and his eye swelled up immediately. They took him off the field, and the ambulance brought him to the hospital. Nevertheless, the game continued.

On defense, I had a really great game. I caught every ball that was in the air and rifled balls back to the bases to get runners out. However, I really made a difference at the plate. After Seb went out of the game and we got back on offense, I hit a homer off of Jimmy, one of my good friends at school. The horns started blasting as I rounded the bases. The whistling air that blew through my helmet was mixed with the cheers and honks. I stomped on home plate with so much delight. My family smiled, my team high fived me and patted me vigorously on the back. After I sat down in the dugout, my coach dropped down to one knee, looked me in the eye and said, "Great hit, Brett! I am proud of you."

His simple words fueled my motivation. Later in the game I hit a line-drive double between left and center. I hustled to second base and just touched it as the defense caught the ball.

"Nice hit Brett!"

"Great running, Brett!"

I heard smatterings of cheers for me throughout the horns and claps. The game was tied, and I wanted so bad to reach home. We had two outs, and I desperately felt the need to make it to third on the next hit.

My teammate, Gavin, Brady's best friend, was a solid hitter. He hit a fast grounder between second and first which drew off the second baseman. I attempted to launch off second, but our third base coach waved me to stay. I ignored him, committed to running to third base no matter what. The second baseman fired the ball to third as Gavin touched first. I realized as the ball reached the third baseman that I was now in a 'pickle,' the game played so many days with my crew in the field. I halted for a moment as the third baseman started moving towards me. I decided I was going to sell the notion of me sprinting back to second. I faked hard going to second, and the third baseman tossed it over my head toward his teammate. I waited for the ball to leave the third baseman's fingertips and reversed direction towards third as hard as I could.

Horns blasted and voices shrieked because I was almost to third as the ball arced in the air. I dove. Every single one of my fingers extended out to get past the dirt and find the plate. That was what I loved about baseball: taking risks like in the pickle.

The next play I made it to home plate, and we won the game. More horns, popcorn, ice cream, and my team congratulating me by forming a high-five-line. It was gratifying to get such positive attention from my family, Mimi, coach and friends for playing so well. The game of Pickle characterized my existence for a period of time. I often felt like I was trying to reach home but struggled to stay out of those precarious and risky situations. They didn't always end so well as that game.

BRADY
Werewolf

The Wizard of Oz was such a big movie when we were growing up. We had to take a nap in order to stay up late and watch it on t.v. It came on once a year. So if you didn't catch it then you had to wait an entire year in order to watch it again. Brett and I would get especially excited to see The Wicked Witch and the Flying Monkeys. He like to pretend to be the Lion, and I would be the Tin Man. Mom would make popcorn for us. Sometimes Mimi or Uncle Phil would stay over, and it was like our own little party.

So when Halloween came and Mimi decided to be the Scarecrow it was not a big surprise. Each year, Mimi being the artist of the family made my brother and me up into some character. She made me into Dracula and colored my skin to look dead and my mouth to look bloody. She slicked back Brett's hair and got him ripped-up clothes and made him a biker gang member. She pulled out all the stops when making her costumes as well. The year she was the Scarecrow, she used real straw and had it sewn into a hat so it came down to cover her face and head. She devised little slits so she could see through the straw. She looked amazing. She would strut around and act floppy like the real Scarecrow would in the movie.

As she constructed our costumes she drank her wine, and people would come in and out of our house to say hello and show off their kids' costumes. This particular Halloween Brett, Mimi and I got ready to go out to trick or treat. After we hit our neighborhood, my mom drove us to Bonus Land, across the highway to the nice houses.

There was this one house across Highway 202 we always tried to trick or treat but chickened out everytime. All the adults knew the guy who lived there and he went all out. He had spooky music playing from speakers in his trees and zombies crawling out of the grass. He had big foot prints going up his driveway around back to the screen door. Every year we followed the footsteps and got to the screen door and rang the doorbell only to see this scary creature come out of the darkness, and like clockwork, we tucked tail and ran back to the car. In the house all the lights were turned off except for a few big candles. There was even creepier music playing in the house. Out of the darkness the werewolf creature staggered out toward the door. He was hairy with fangs. Even his hands and feet had claws and fur. Seeing him hunched over and starting to growl sent us and all the real little kids running. The adults laughed and encouraged us to give it another try. For years when we were little we never had the nerve to stay.

The first year I finally did it was amazing. We got around back, and the werewolf started to get real close. My brother had already turned and ran back, but I was determined. As the werewolf made it to the screen door, his clawed index finger curled to invite me to enter. At all the other houses the person just came to the door and gave us candy after the trick or treat phrase. Not the werewolf. He made me step a foot inside the screen door, and I faintly said, "trick or treat."

He held out a plastic pumpkin, daring me to reach inside.

I grabbed the first thing my fingertips touched, said, "thank you," and sprinted to the car all in one fluid movement. When I finally got to the car, I heard Brett say, "Holy Cow that thing is huge!"

As I sat in the car, I looked down into the palm of my sweaty hands to view the prize: a full size Snickers bar. It wasn't one of the mini size bars that every single house gave out. It was four times the size of those. It was just like the ones you would buy in the store when it wasn't Halloween season.

"Aw, man, I should have stayed," Brett moaned.

"Maybe next year Brett," my mother encouraged.

I just sat there smiling at my full size candy bar with such joy.

For the last stop we always went to my Aunt Deena's neighborhood. She was the real reason Mimi got all dressed up. Aunt Deena was one of my Mimi's sisters, and for years when we went to her house for Halloween the game was for Mimi to try and trick Aunt Deena into not knowing her own sister. Mimi was so good with the costumes that many times Aunt Deena just thought she was another high school kid who couldn't give up on the Halloween tradition.

After all the wine and excitement, we finally got to Aunt Deena's street. My mom suggested that Brett and I trick or treat at the neighbor's house before going to Aunt Deena's because this was the last stop. We would usually all go in and visit for a bit as the grand finale for the night.

I don't know if it was the excitement of whether or not we could trick Aunt Deena or Mimi just had too much wine, but as we got up to the neighbor's house, Mimi thought we were actually at Aunt Deena's. She was a little wobbly from the wine, and she couldn't see very well with the straw in her face. When the unsuspecting neighbor opened the door and we all yelled 'trick or treat,' Mimi realized it wasn't her sister who answered the door. Mimi burst into the house giggling and laughing.

"Where is she?"

"Deena?"

The neighbor was in shock.

"Mimi, this isn't the house," we told her.

"Oh, sorry," she said as she gave the nice man a big hug.

Giggling and carrying on, Brett and I escorted Mimi next door where she could properly say 'trick or treat' to her sister, who had no clue it was her.

My mother parked the car and we all piled into her house. Aunt Deena gave my brother and me the customary hard pinch on the cheeks, which was her welcoming gesture to the kids in her family.

The adults visited and drank some more as Brett and I laid out our candy to view our loot. We spread everything out and make trades for the things we liked the most. That year was the best because sitting on my pile like the biggest brick of gold was the full bar of Snickers.

Some kids might have got more candy that night, but I didn't care. In fact, I was a lot more generous with the trades I made with Brett. Most years with me being older I could con him out of some of the candy that I really wanted. This year, however, I didn't care about the pile quite the same. It was all about the one big bar. The satisfaction of braving the werewolf long outlasted the Snickers.

BRETT
This was designed for me

A s I woke up on a sunny summer morning, I quickly got dressed and bolted for the door. This was my routine on those long summer days: Get out of bed as fast as I could, maybe brush my teeth, jump on my BMX bike and peddle up and down Maple Street. I hit every jump, launching off every curb, and doing wheelies as far down the road as I could hold them. That was my ritual while I waited for the neighborhood kids to come out. I put myself on display, trying to entice any of my friends to break from the TV and get outside. Brady, Ben, Kevin.....I would stalk back and forth nonstop waiting for someone to play. I could do it until the sun went down.

I was not interested in TV or Atari. That stuff bored me. Sitting down made me crazy. I would jump at the chance to go play ball, though. Brady and I would try to get as many people as possible. Between his friends and him,, me and mine and then anyone else from the neighborhood, it wasn't long before something got going. It always did.

I loved to jump in the games with the older guys. It didn't matter if it was baseball or tackle football where I got my ass kicked. I was always excited to mix it up with the high schoolers. Playing with them felt like getting called up to the Major Leagues. They only let younger kids play if they knew you could play. I could play. I envisioned the ballfield as Candlestick Park. The eyes of the crowd were on me. They wanted to know what I was going to do next. This was my proving ground.

Fall was football season. As the morning burned into afternoon I got 'called up' with my friend Ben. Most likely we wouldn't get many plays, but the fact that we got to play football was all that mattered. The older guys did not go easy on us. We would get tossed around. Mixing it up meant getting slammed into the hard-ass ground by guys twice our size whenever we tried to make a block. The game moved along, and Ben and I were merely pin balls ricocheting around at the high school kids' commands. Ben and I were constantly reminded that we were the little guys on this field.

Then, towards the end of the game, David, who was the captain for my team, suggested a post route that he had taught me the previous week.

"Brett, if you are open - you are going to get it," he whispered.

My heart jumped to my throat. I was so excited. I was not afraid. Every part of me knew I could make this play. The crowd in my head was watching me. That whole game I had just waited for the chance to prove myself. Making a successful play in front of the older guys and getting their approval was everything to me. In fact, at that moment it was the only thing I wanted.

The huddle broke. Could the guys on the other side hear my heart pounding? I remember thinking that if they did, then they would know the ball was coming straight to me. On the other hand, I was considered the least likely to receive the ball. The game was close, and usually us little guys received no love in close games: blowouts sure, but I wanted to be the go-to-guy in the nail-biter.

"Hut one, hut two, hut three!" David called out without a change in cadence.

As we ran the play, I sprinted down the field as hard as my legs would take me. Ben and I mostly covered each other, but we always got clipped by an older guy (a reminder that we were with the big boys). My heart was louder than my footsteps. Brian hit me hard a few steps off the line of scrimmage, which left Ben as the only one pursuing me. I stayed on my feet and kept hauling ass. I planted my foot in the ground and dug in to make my cut. That left Ben a couple steps behind. As I broke to the post, I glanced over my right shoulder, and watched David launch the ball.

It was designed for me. The ball soared in the air. Everyone knew David had the best arm around. The ball had a perfect spiral. I listened to the pros on TV say that when they had great games time slowed down. It sure did. As the ball moved through the air, everything else faded: my Dad's pissed off voice, my homework. The slow silence was all that was left. However, the silence ended abruptly when the opposing team caught on.

"Holy shit, this ball is for Brett!"

By then it was too late. They all were too far away. They were beat. Ben was now four steps behind. The older guys started cussing. Inside my head I stated confidently, "That's right. This ball is mine."

I kept my eyes locked on that ball. A rock to the face was not going to make me even blink. I was going to make this play! It hit me in perfect stride. As soon as the ball reached my hands, I brought it in safely, cradled it, protected it...because there was no way I was dropping this one. The cursing turned to cheering. The guys on my team screamed and jumped. I raced to the end zone and scored.

My life was always so hectic. There were so many things I didn't understand. The things that I did understand, I couldn't tolerate. But this moment was perfect. Following the ball towards my fingertips and feeling the football secured in my hands felt unbelievably gratifying. The guys piled on me. They smacked me and Ben around all day, but as all those big bodies crushed me into that grass, I smiled. We paid our dues and that play made it worthwhile.

As my scrawny body squished toward the ground, I thought, "Today I proved it. This play was designed for me and I did it."

BRADY
Shane

When I was really young and my Mom and the Old Man were still together, they invested in a tiny cabin out in the woods. It had no electricity or running water and we drove down a long dirt road to get to it. The second floor was all beds and cots. A ton of people could stay up there with us, and when they did we had some fun. My Uncle and Mimi would come up with cousins and all kinds of my parents' friends. Our black lab, Shane, was always running around the perimeter of the property. He was an outside dog because I was severely allergic to fur, so my mom would not let him come in the house. Shane loved being up at the cabin because he could run free.

We played board games at night, made bonfires, roasted marshmallows, and cranked around on a go-cart. Some of the best times I can remember as a really little kid were at that cabin. There were a few times we even had a few laughs with the Old Man before he got really bad. The adults partied like crazy, and us kids scurried around everywhere.

Shane was a great dog. He followed my brother, cousins and me all around when we were at the cabin. He didn't get to run around as much at our house. In fact, old neighbor Johnnie would walk him every day with all of his dogs. Johnnie was good like that; he took care of any animals that needed taking care of. The cabin was totally different. Shane loped all over the place, coming back with burrs and porcupine quills in his hair, and occasionally smelling like a skunk. Thunderstorms were the only thing that crashed his party. He darted under the safety of the cabin porch at the sound of thunder.

One summer the Old Man had his arm in a sling due to an infection in his hand. He had cut his knuckle on some guy's tooth while punching him in the face at a bar. The Old Man always came back with scrapes and welts from bar brawls. Growing up with that man around was touchy because he went from being really nice to really mean in a second. When he started drinking, it was just best to steer clear.

Being so far out in the woods, some of the men sat around and shot their guns off at cans and bottles. City rules did not apply way out here. The kids chilled behind and off to the side and watched them target practice. It was a thrill to see who was good enough to hit the targets from a distance. My mom didn't like shooting too much because everyone usually drank, and I was sure she didn't think mixing those two things together was smart. She also didn't like how the cracking of the guns freaked Shane out. It made him go crazy. He would howl nonstop during thunderstorms, so we would bring him in the basement so he wouldn't have a complete meltdown. After the first couple shots were fired, he yelped and then tucked tail to bury himself under the porch. One particular evening, the Old Man got drunk as usual, but initially remained in a pretty good mood. He laughed and carried on with all the adults. He brought out his rifle and lined up some cans to shoot. When the tone of voices coming from the adults started to get serious toward the end of the afternoon, we stopped playing a game of hide and seek.

My Uncle called me 'ears' sometimes because he claimed I had sonar hearing. When the adults talked about stuff the kids were not supposed to hear, I always tuned in to see if I could catch bits and pieces. The key to tuning in didn't start with the words, but with the tone. So we all stood off in the distance and watched as the other adults started reprimanding the Old Man.

"You are half in the bag, man, now is not the time to shoot that thing!"

"Your hand is still swollen. You don't want to go and do that."

"The kick back of the gun is going to hurt your hand like a son of a bitch."

Like so many times, the Old Man was not hearing any of it. He lined up the sights and squeezed the trigger. Not only did he miss the target but dropped the gun.

"Shit!" He hopped around holding his hand. "Son of a...!"

Smiles and laughs vanished. The Old Man was pissed. He cussed more. He stormed around attempting to set up more bottles to prove that he could hit something. My Uncle Phil tried to reason with him. Most of the other adults acted like the kids and just cleared the way. We all had seen this side of the Old Man too often.

Then for no apparent reason he started to call Shane.

"Shane!" he shouted.

"Shane! Come here boy!"

My mom stood on the porch and said, "Leave the poor thing alone. You know how he gets."

"That damn dog is to come when I call it."

Why the Old Man went from hell bent on shooting bottles and cans to demanding Shane by his side was anyone's guess. Everyone knew the dog hid and shook when those guns went off. But this is what the Old Man did. Instead of leaving Shane alone, he had to torment him while he was scared out of his mind. He insisted the poor dog come out from under the cabin right after he shot the gun. In fact, he shot it off some more just to deepen the torture.

"The fuckin' dog better come out!"

Some of the adults sheepishly protested.

"Just leave him alone."

"He is scared."

Nothing stopped the Old Man. It never did. He waved that gun around and yelled Shane's name more. The Old Man marched towards the porch.

"I will get that fuckin' thing to come out."

Seeing him b-line towards the cabin made my Uncle bolt toward him knowing that the scene most likely would get uglier. The escalation in the Old Man's temper also made my mother frantically wave us into the side door. In a matter of seconds the Old Man was crouched by the porch where Shane hid, screaming and waving his gun at the dog.

Every kid, including me, was flat out hysterical because we were convinced our dog was about to be killed. Some adults cried, some prayed and some yelled from inside for the Old Man to stop. We all took cover.

The Old Man never shot Shane. Just as quickly the idea of calling Shane from under the porch entered his mind and distracted him from shooting more bottles, so did the idea of going to the bar distract him from shooting our dog. After a mere few minutes of bending over cursing and waving the rifle at the dog, the Old Man just threw the rifle on the porch, jumped into The Green Hornet and peeled off.

Like the Munchkins in Munchkin Land after the Wicked Witch left, we slowly started to poke our heads out. Some came out the front door, some from under covers and some just peeked out a window. As the dust from the Old Man's car settled and my Uncle peered down the 'Yellow Brick Road,' he finally yelled to everyone's relief.

"He's gone!"

BRETT
Red Flags

Mimi would have massive Christmas Parties with our family and friends every year on Princeton Street. The Kerry family lived a few doors down. Princeton Street was a dead end and really close to Parker's Pond where we would skate in the winter time. A line of cars bordered the hill Christmas Eve. Mrs. Kerry was one of Mimi's best friends and had a huge family. Most of her male relatives were avid hunters and fishermen. Dave married into the Kerry family, and when he began coming to the Christmas Parties I took to him right away. He was a prison guard at one of the state prisons in the area, and I remember thinking what a tough life dealing with hardened criminals all day must be. Dave was such a stoic guy. He was always calm and relaxed.

"What is working in the prison like?" I asked.

"It has its ups and downs." I could tell he was purposely vague.

"What do you do?" I was literally at the edge of my seat.

"Well, I work with the K-9 Unit," he merely said.

"What the heck is that?"

Dave went on to describe how the dogs he trained helped patrol and sniff out contraband within the prison. After he described what contraband was, Dave continued to tell me what his day was like working with prison guard dogs. I thought that being able to work with such well-trained animals was incredible. He recounted the exercises that they did to keep the dogs sharp and the bond that the handlers formed with 'their' dogs.

After seeing Dave over a few holidays Mimi prompted him to take Brady and me ice fishing. Brady and I fished a lot, but we were amateurs. We would dig worms and go down to the Three Pipes hoping to get a nibble. Dave was a true sport fisherman, so when he picked us up on an early Saturday morning in his big, jacked-up Dodge Power Wagon, I could barely sit still. Ice fishing was a concept that we didn't quite understand. Brady and I drilled him with questions the entire drive there.

"How are we going to get the fish through the ice?"

"Aren't the fish sleeping under the ice?"

"Boys," Dave said calmly in a deep voice. "Settle down. When we get there I will show you how it is done. I will warn you -- you both will have to be patient."

Thank goodness mom dressed us like we were going sledding. We had on our snow pants and our snow boots. We argued with her when she suggested all the layers, but as soon as we got out of the truck by the open ice, the blast of frigid air made us understand in a hurry why she insisted we put on so much clothing.

Dave instructed us to put some of the gear on sleds, and we jumped to it. I hustled around to fetch, grab or lift anything Dave requested. I was determined to listen because I wanted to catch something. The idea of pulling a fish out from under the thick wall of ice seemed miraculous. We hiked out on the ice for a long time. A few times Brady and I looked at each other wondering, "What the hell did we get ourselves into." We walked straight into a steady gust of wind that stiffened us up and required us to lean in order to make any forward progress. White flakes swirled all around us, making visibility low. As we got towards the middle of the lake, all we could make out was white. If I squinted I could barely see the tree line at the shore.

When Dave began drilling holes we got our smiles back. We turned our backs to the wind and watched the spiral carve into the ice. Two or three times I looked at Brady in disbelief that the drill had not reached the open water yet. When it finally did, my brother and I cheered. After several holes were drilled fifty feet or so apart, Dave pulled out the rigs that we would use to fish. It was a foreign contraption with a red flag at the end that would supposedly pop up when a fish hit it. Dave made my brother and me bait our own hooks by feeding the point through the minnows lip.

"You want to have the hook just behind the lip so the minnow stays alive and flits around. That is going to attract the big ones," he explained.

Brady and I were all ears. We nodded and did everything Dave told us to do. After a few minutes we had our lines loaded with bait. Now he told us we had to wait. As Dave was 'jigging' or whatever he called it, my brother and I took to running around and tackling each other. Dave said that was fine as long as we didn't do it near him because he was fishing 'by hand' out of this one hole." He just sat motionless on an upside-down bucket, stared at his line and occasionally looked up as us grinning.

Dave struck a nice balance of letting Brady and me blow off steam on the open ice while helping us still understand that we were also there to fish. "You both have to watch your own flags. I am not going to tell you if they go up," he warned.

Brett and I each had TWO flags to watch! That meant two holes. As we tackled, tripped, and rolled around the open ice, time meandered by. It took a long time for the first flag to spring, but my brother and I didn't mind. I think I had Brady in a head-lock when the first flag went up. And it was mine.

"Aw, Crap!!" I yelled when I saw my flag pop-up. I released my brother's head and sprinted over to my rig.

"Dave! What do I do?"

Dave came over and showed me how to reel the fish up. I could feel the beast pulling in different directions -- jerking the line back and forth. Dave helped me finess it through the hole, and it was a big pickerel. The creature thrashed on the top of the ice as if looking for the hole. Brady and I gasped. The pickerel was beautiful with shimmering colors.

"That is a nice fish kiddo!" Dave said with a pat on my back.

This was by far the biggest fish I had ever caught in my entire life. In fact Brady and I caught a few more that day, and all of them were keeper pickerels. Playing on the ice while waiting for those flags to shoot up was such a great day. One time both Brady's and my flags went up almost at the exact same time. We were in heaven. Gone were the biting wind, icy hands, and numb cheeks. By the time we packed everything up, my brother and I were roasting and smiling.

The whole ride home was filled with fish stories. We rehashed the adventure of who caught the biggest fish, who got the best of each other when we wrestled in between flags going up. The whole time Dave laughed and congratulated us equally.

"You both did a great job."

"I would fish with you guys anytime," he chuckled.

Unfortunately, we never got the chance to go ice fishing again. I suppose we moved around and life just got in the way. However, the perfection of that day is etched into my mind: the clear crisp air, the swirling snow, and how the red flags would stand up and make my brother and me scream to a halt and dash over to them. Those red flags signaled something exciting on the other end of those lines that held our imagination.

BRADY
Ice Capades

B y the time I was about to reach middle school the Old Man was in such a bad state that he got on a kick of using my brother and me to hurt my mother. He came to our school several times while Mom was at work, to try and take us out of school without permission, but the principal would not let him. There were instances where he strong-armed our babysitters to relinquish guardianship. One night we hid up in my Auntie Ju's attic as he forced his way into her apartment looking for us. She stood her ground and was able to refute his advances by convincing him there was no glaring evidence of us being in her apartment. Friends and neighbors would call my mother if they saw the Green Hornet prowling around. My mother was in constant fear that he would smuggle us away while she was at work. She had finally obtained a restraining order against him being within a certain distance of us and the house, but the Old Man wasn't worried about that. The Hornet would appear, and if the opportunity of a snatch and grab seemed futile, the Hornet would vanish before the cops came.

After the night in Auntie Ju's attic, the Old Man did not come around for a long time. It was probably the longest stint we had gone without seeing him. In fact, it had been so long that our lives were starting to seem normal.

The string of normalcy in our lives allowed mom to take us to Parker's Pond. Mom loved to ice skate. She would take us to Mimi's house, and we would walk down to Parker's Pond, and she would do figure eights and skate backwards while Brett and I would race around and smash into one another. My mom rarely showed the level of joy and freedom that she did when she cut around on Parker's Pond. She would describe how she had skated there as a kid with her friends.

Because of this love, she purchased some tickets for her, my Auntie Ju, Brett, and me to see Ice Capades. The show would have these big name skaters with cartoon characters skating around doing funny stuff. We never skated or organized fun trips like this when the Old Man was around. This night was big time. The tickets were expensive, we had to drive over an hour to see the show, and we would get back in the middle of the night. My Mom was really excited about this adventure.

The show was pretty cool. I had never seen anything like it. The four of us got lost in the lights, the crowd, and the sound. Everything was amplified, drowning out our dusty life in the neighborhood. My Aunt and my mother were kids again sitting alongside my brother and me.

During the long drive home, Brett and I fell asleep. Auntie Ju and Mom had to carry each of us into the house. When we got through the doorway, the slumber that covered us was ripped away.

"Shit," my Aunt whispered. Although she didn't say it loud, it was her tone that woke us up in an instant.

The four of us stood in the doorway in disbelief. The house was completely destroyed. Not one item was in its original place, and anything that could be broken was broken. Major furniture was overturned, pictures on the wall were knocked off, and everything from every shelf was ripped or destroyed. It was no mystery that the Old Man had done the damage, and since the front door was left open when we approached, we was assumed he was gone.

As we walked further into the house it was clear that he treated each room equally. However, there was this sense of relief. The rearranged house where every material object was destroyed was fine because the Old Man seemed to be absent.

We were about to enter the kitchen when we heard a creak up in the attic. Thank goodness Auntie Ju was there because the three of us had endured so much of the Old Man's antics that we were about to go into panic mode.

"Ok, boys get washed up," Auntie Ju said in a nice loud voice. She turned to us and gestured to stay calm. She walked toward the folded attic stairs, but instead of pulling them down she let them snap up. The only way to the attic were stairs folded into the ceiling. We had to jump up and pull a ring to bring them down and then straighten the ladder out to touch the floor. Because my mom was so small, she always folded the ladder half way and left the trap door open so she didn't have to jump up and grab the ring each time. The Old Man had crawled up to the attic and somehow folded the ladder behind him to make us think no one was up there.

Now that the trapdoor in the ceiling was closed, Auntie Ju got on the phone and called the cops. She used a broom and a chair to brace against the door just in case the Old Man wanted to get tricky and force his way down.

The police were at our house in minutes. We listened for any noise the whole time we waited and heard nothing. The two officers had us step back as they uncoiled the ladder.

As the four of us huddled together and the first policeman slowly made his way up the rickety ladder with his flashlight and gun drawn, I noticed the Green Hornet tucked far behind The Shop behind our house.

The first cop called out the Old Man's name as he continued up the stairs but got no response. When he got up to the attic, the other followed. We could hear muffled voices and then a scuffle. Soon they brought the Old Man down in cuffs. One braced him and frisked him while the other bagged a pistol. As the cops made sure he had no other weapons, the Old Man just stared at us with this smirk. His jeering grin suggested he was getting away with something and did not have a care in the world. His bottomless black eyes locked on to my mother as she and my Aunt stood between us and him. He could barely walk, however, his stare was steady. The Old Man's glare burrowed into my welled-up eyes and created a tremor throughout my whole body.

As the cops began to march him out the front door, he knelt down in front of me. The policeman gripped his shoulder, his hands were behind his back, the booze oozed from his breath and his eyes were level with mine.

"Always remember who the man of the house is," he grumbled at me.

The officer hoisted him up with an intolerant jerk and took the Old Man away.

BRETT
Something to Prove

B rady ran cross country and track in high school. He was really good. Sometimes he let me hang with his high school friends, and I wanted to prove I was worthy of tagging along. My mom liked me hanging around with my brother because he was a good influence at this time in my life. I was constantly in trouble and my brother was not. I started to feel as if I was worth less than he was. The neighbors would cut out clippings from the paper of some races where Brady was named or pictured. My mother started a scrapbook with all the clippings. Sometimes we would get multiple clippings in the mailbox because people down the street seemed randomly to send them to her.

I always tried to make some impact in sports to garner the attention that Brady earned with his running. It didn't matter if it was football, basketball or even pole vaulting. I wanted to make people stop and take notice of me. To compound matters, my mom threatened to take sports away if I didn't keep my grades up, so I was always at war with myself, fighting this internal battle to do the right thing and to try and excel.

When I was young Michael Jordan was showing the world how dunking the basketball was something of an art form. Being five feet eight inches tall, I was often told that I would never be able to dunk. One summer, some landscape guys were working on the yard. I made a ramp from the skids that they used to haul big plants on. I used it as a jump to assist in my pursuit of dunking the ball. I practiced for hours. I gradually took one board at a time away from the ramp until I just needed merely one or two to jump off and dunk. I dreamed vicious dunk executions. I imagined the crowd going wild. Many times the ball bounced off the back iron in defeat. If my timing wasn't right, I might get the height off the ramp but still miss the dunk, but all summer, I just kept jumping and jumping.

"I will flush that ball hard," I said to myself. I pictured a defender in front of me as I made a couple moves to get by him and drive to the hoop.

Towards the end of that summer I achieved the height without the ramp and just needed to improve the timing and ball control. The landscapers sometimes stopped the work they were doing, leaned on their shovels, and watched me with grins on their faces. Having an audience, no matter how small, motivated me. I wanted to show anyone interested that I could do it. One day, as they stopped for lunch sitting on their coolers all ready to watch me I got amped up. I dribbled to the hoop, took my two steps and launched. As I elevated, I knew instantly I was going to get the height. I needed to focus and time it just right. I cocked my arm back while controlling the ball and smashed it right in the hoop.

Bang! I came down.

I could hear the guys say, "Did you see that?"

I swelled up with pride. Not only did I do it, but I did it with an audience. The landscapers came over and congratulated me, "Nice work man."

All those afternoons of jumping off my training ramp paid off. As days went by, I perfected my dunk. I was able to do it at will more and more often.

Finally, Brady and his friend Keith pulled up after a morning of training. As they walked down the driveway after parking the car on the street, I yelled out, "Hey guys, watch this!"

I skyed in the air and slammed down the perfect dunk. I let out a howl as my feet came back to the ground. They stood in the driveway with their mouths wide open.

"Damn, man, nice job!"

"Seeing you need that ramp all summer, we never thought you would ever do it by yourself!"

Keith was especially impressed because he played on our school's basketball team. He used to crunch me in our one-on-one games the previous summer. Witnessing his and my brother's faces when I dunked again to prove it wasn't luck was sweet as heck. I had some solid basketball games in high school. I had a couple games where I scored as much as 41 points, but that experience of executing a dunk in front of my brother and his friend has to rank up there as one of my most treasured sporting memories. From listening to them heckle me relentlessly early in the summer while I fumbled around with my ramp, to the day when their doubting faces dropped in disbelief, I had proved myself.

BRADY
Promises, Promises

When our father was taken away it was just the three of us. My Mom was working two jobs, so she asked our Uncle Phil to come stay in our house. Mom billed this arrangement a my brother and me needing a 'positive male role model." However, my brother and I understood he was here to keep us in line. We were growing older, and her Wooden Spoon was not having the desired effect it once did. We were getting bigger, and the Wooden Spoon was getting smaller, so Mom waving it around wasn't as intimidating anymore.

Uncle Phil drove his blue van across the country from California with his surfboard tied to the top. Having Uncle Phil back was amazing. He was around when we were really young and the family used to have the Camp and we would fish and go hiking with him on weekends. Uncle Phil had moved out to California not long after. We would send him Polaroid pictures while he would send us letters that would describe his surfing and the California sun. My mom would read the letters as Mimi, Brett, and I would

87

gather around to listen to his experiences in such a foreign place. Having him back, even though he was coming back to lay down the law for Brett and me, was great. His curiosity excited us. Uncle Phil made a point to take us hiking, exploring, driving around surrounding towns, fishing, and any whim that seemed to pop into his mind. We idolized his sense of adventure and how he made us feel like his time with us was special to him.

After the first couple days he sat the two of us down and explained the 'ground rules.' Up until that day there was a slight possibility that we were getting away with a lot. Mom was working serious hours, and we ran around with a lot of freedom. Some of the bad stuff that we might have done never made it back to my mother. So unless we got sent to the principal's office and school called home, my mom wasn't privy to what we were doing. Now in fourth grade, Brett was getting calls home for fighting or disrupting, so began the conversation of us making better decisions.

"Ok, Boys, you are starting with a clean slate," Uncle Phil started explaining as directly as possible.

"I love you two, so I expect from here on out that you behave in school and stay out of trouble. I am here to help your Mother out. So I am going to promise you now that if you do not behave, I will be the one punishing you. I don't want to have to do it, so please do not put me in that position."

Our Uncle had always been the 'fun guy,' so listening to him be serious and taking on a role where he would be the one putting the hurt on us if we messed up was bizarre.

"Uncle Phil, we will be good. We promise," both of us stated in the most sincere way. The last thing that we wanted to do was to disappoint our Uncle.

We were doing well for a few weeks, and then my mother got a call from one of Brett's teachers because he was messing around in class.

That following night my Uncle sat Brett down in the parlor, as I sat in the kitchen in perfect ear shot and tuned into the conversation.

"Brett I warned you that you were going to get punished if you got in trouble."

"I know Uncle Phil," Brett said in his little voice.

"This is going to be your last warning. If you get in trouble one more time I am going to have to punish you, and I can promise you it is not going to be comfortable. I don't want to have to do this so keep your nose clean."

"I am sorry Uncle Phil. I promise I won't do anything again."

As I listened I knew for sure that Uncle Phil would follow through with what he said, and I knew for sure that I would not mess up and that there was a very good possibility Brett was going to slip up. It wasn't like he tried to screw up - it was more like he had trouble keeping his emotions in check.

Unfortunately, it didn't take long, and sure enough the call came from school: Brett got caught fighting again.

So as they did just weeks ago, Uncle Phil and Brett sat in the parlor, and I perked up my ears in the kitchen.

"Brett, I don't understand. I warned you, and now I have to carry out the punishment. This is going to hurt me more than it is going to hurt you." He marched Brett down to the basement. There was a long pause. Then I could hear this sharp smack of a belt on what I could only guess was across Brett's butt. There was another gap of silence then the second smack.

Three, then Four.....The hits came in a perfect cadence with no sound in between. My first thought was that the belt was hitting the wall and not my brother because all I could hear was the snap. Then Five, pause, and Six, then the whimpers started. Seven, Eight the whimpers turned to cries. When Nine and Ten came in perfect rhythm, as if Uncle Phil was following a metronome, Brett was flat out screaming and begging for my Uncle to stop. The tenth one was the last. It was so hard to hear my brother cry like that, in between the harsh cracks of the belt, that I had to fight to keep the tears from welling up in my eyes.

"Brett, that was so hard for me to do. I hope that you will make a better decision next time because I don't want to have to do this again."

"Ok Uncle Phil," Brett whimpered with that skippy way of talking that kids get when they are crying really hard.

I pretended to be doing something as Uncle Phil came upstairs. His eyes had a melancholy flatness to them. The smile that always seemed etched into his face was gone. It was at that moment that I really started to understand that the dumb-ass stuff we did hurt the adults who loved us. It really did hurt him to whip my brother. Unlike in the Old Man's eyes where I would see contempt, with my Uncle or my Mother I detected a deeper angst. On that day I made a promise to myself to try not to cause them hurt.

BRETT
The Village

The summer before my freshman year Brady and I went to a new Training Village in the western part of the state. I begged my mom to go. A former NFL player named Mr. Billick gave a presentation to our school about how he trained really hard as a slow fat kid and eventually made it to the Pros! I figured if I worked really hard like he did maybe I could make it to the NFL someday too. My mother made Brady go with me because she thought it would be good for him. Brady was not happy about giving up six weeks of his summer to go with me to this camp, but he couldn't get out of it. Arguing with my mom when she had her mind set was futile. The Training Village was supposed to mirror boot camp in the military by teaching us discipline, making us work hard, and bettering our skills as athletes. It was a six-week-gig that was supposed to get us 'at risk' kids to stay on track during summer and ready for the fall sport we would play. I didn't care about all that; I just wanted to have a chance to make it some place playing football.

At the Training Village we had to get up at 4:30 in the morning and be out on the road running by 5:00 am. The counselors would line us up across this lonely country road and send us off into the steamy morning air. We ran in full sweats with a short towel around our necks like the old boxers did. Mr. Billick, the founder of the Training Village, was a former running back for the Patriots back in the 60s, and he adopted his training methods from some guy he had met in his youth. The idea was we would get up before everyone else did and be working while the rest of the world slept. All day we had activities that were geared towards making us faster, stronger, and tougher. So 30 of us high school boys would be out on the roads before sane people were up running a hilly 9-mile loop every morning. It was basically a race every day, and my darn brother won every time and would be showered before the rest of us even finished. These runs were miserable. It was hot, the full sweats were heavy, and this loop was long.

One morning I began my sufferfest as usual while thinking to myself how much I hated running. I was only halfway done with the treachery. I was thirsty after just completing the monster hill that was like climbing Everest every morning and now had to travel down the last drawn-out stretch on highway 64. I had passed Clem's Diner over and over again during these runs. After two weeks of passing Clem's, on this particularly blazing hot morning, I decided it was worth the risk to go into Clem's to ask for some water and take a short break.

I had already been in trouble a few times with Mr. Billick for fighting and not listening to the counselors. I felt bad about my shenanigans because he was such a great guy.

He would sit me down and say, "What are you thinking Big Guy?"

"If you want to get better, you can't take short cuts."

"You're killing me Big Guy."

"I don't want to have to let you go, but you can't be doing that Brett."

Campers were threatened with being kicked out if they didn't toe the line on basic rules. Mr. Billick was a pillar in the Boston community who was known to all of us as a giving and patient man. However, even Mr. Billick was losing patience with me.

Nevertheless, my thirst outweighed any fear of consequences at this point. The customary bell on the door announced my presence in the dusty old diner. The three customers turned to stare me down. Clem was behind the counter.

"What can I do for you, young man?"

"Could I get a glass of water please?"

Clem responded with a gentle smile, "coming right up."

As he slid the glass along the counter, he asked, "How is your run going? I see you boys out there pounding the pavement every morning. That is good for you. It reminds me of my days in the military. That Mr. Billick is quite the man."

"Yeah," I grunted as I pounded the water. "Thanks, I better get back on the road."

"Any time, but I suppose they don't want you stoppin' because then all the boys would be in here." Clem chuckled. "Like I said, I think it's great seeing you boys out there working out."

"Thanks again," I responded with one foot out the door. I was already scanning the street for other runners so as not to be detected. I had lost a little bit of time so I immediately thought of my plan B. Over the last couple weeks I had also spotted a set of railroad tracks that in my scheming mind obviously cut through the landscape and conveniently divided the course in half. I could jog a little and walk a little and easily get back on track in no time by just following those. It would cut the distance I had to run in half. I made sure to jump into the spot behind Peter, the camper I was behind before Clem's, as he passed by the tracks without seeing me.

When I reached the road and finished up without being detected I was so happy. My shortcut worked out so well that I did that method a few more times. I also got bolder and started hitching rides along highway 64 which really got me down the road fast. I was trouble free for a couple weeks. Until I was not. Word got out to the campers about what I was doing and the rumors spread.

Mr. Billick called me into his office during lunch one day.

"Big guy, I gave you so many chances and you know I love you."

With my head hung low I merely muttered, "yeah."

"You are just not giving me any choices here. We can't have you continue at the Village if you keep breaking the rules like this. You are angry, Big Guy, I can see that. But we love you - you know that don't you?"

"Yeah," I started sobbing. I don't know why. I just felt so bad. Mr. Billick was such a good guy, but man, this running early in the morning was so hard. I hated letting him down. I begged him not to kick me out. He mentioned something about my brother doing so well, and that we only had a few days left, but that I had to be better the last few days.

I agreed not only to be better but to be great, and I did squeak by without any huge problem. I got in a minor tussle with one kid in the bunkhouse, but we all were able to keep it from the counselors.

I was so happy that I didn't get kicked out because the last night we had a banquet, and they gave out awards. Brady got something for killing the run every morning. I didn't get anything; I knew I wouldn't. But my mom was so happy seeing us complete the six-week 'training camp.' This felt like an extensive journey of army cots, dead legs, hungry stomachs, and pain. And even though I knew I cut corners a lot during my stay, I was proud to be a part of it - for me that was significant. When the counselors described to the audience all that we had done, and I could see my mom sitting straight and smiling in her chair, I was so thankful that I made it through.

BRADY
Bless You

After the cops dragged the Old Man away, a few years went by, and my mother started dating. She kept him from my brother and me until it started getting more serious. Adults will sometimes do that to spare their kids having to get to know people who may not be in their lives for more than a few months. I have to admit that when we found out that she had a new man in her life we weren't too happy. Finally not having the Old Man around had brought us to a place where we seemed to have some normalcy, and we were getting used to just the three of us.

But my mom was excited to finally introduce us 'barbarians' to Mike so deep down we knew the relationship meant a lot to her.

"Now I am inviting Dr. Hartong over for dinner so you all can meet, and I need you two to behave." Mom lectured us on how to act at the table, to be on our best behavior, to not talk with our mouths full, and a bunch of other stuff we never did on a normal day. Dr. Hartong was the surgeon who had taken out Brett's stitches when he got his finger stuck in the manhole cover, so Brett was excited to see him again. Brett hated the guy who set and stitched up his hand but had liked Dr. Hartong when he met him to get his stitches out.

When the Doctor came cruising into our neighborhood with a black Porsche, our whole group of friends stopped the game that we were playing and cleared the street and just stared. Like Rocky running up the stairs in Philly we all ran after the car as it slowly pulled into our driveway. We all stood at the end of our dirt drive-way as this Porsche parked at *our* house. Ben, Kevin, Charlie, and everyone just gazed, with their jaws open, at this magnificent car. We would never see cars like this in our neighborhood or in the town for that matter. But here it was in our driveway, and the driver wasn't lost. It made Brett and me feel like movie stars. After all, this was a far cry from the Green Hornet.

As Dr. Hartong stepped out of the Porsche with his tie and jacket we all straightened up and said, "Hello."

"Hello kids," he said. "What were you all playing?"

"Kickball," we replied in unison.

He walked over to us and stuck out his hand, "You must be Brady and Brett."

We shook his hand and told him all the other kids' names.

"Well, I will see you boys inside," he went to join my mom in the house.

As soon as the door closed we surrounded the Porsche. It didn't have a scratch on it and was the coolest car I had ever seen. You would have thought a spaceship had landed. Other than pictures none of us had ever seen a car like this in real life. The closest was Mr. Hainey at the edge of town who owned the used-car dealer-ship. He had a collection of Corvettes.

Soon after the kids headed home, and Brett and I went inside to clean up and get ready for my mother's big dinner. We were hav-ing steak, and we didn't get steak very often so that was a bonus.

As the four of us sat around the counter together, Dr. Hartong fired off simple questions directed at Brett and me.

"How is school?"

"What is your favorite subject?"

"What sport do you play?"

We answered as politely as we could. My mother's eyes never left us. She was constantly monitoring us with a look that said, "I am watching you two so don't say or do anything stupid."

We were halfway through the meal, and everything seemed to be going well. Then my mother casually sneezed. That is when the wheels came off of our nice dinner. You see, my mother never casually sneezed. She was a legend in our family for these long, winding build ups to machine gun style sneezes that were epic. She would inhale in a deep choppy manner and then explode a succession of outbursts that would scream out one after the other. Sometimes a family member would rub her back and sarcastically say, "It is all right Kath." Sometimes Brett and I would jokingly duck when she would sneeze and she would laugh and tell us to stop it. Her sneezes were loud, funny, and she had done it that way for as long as anyone could remember.

But this time there was no build up; it was just one tiny chirp. That was it. No long warning that it was coming and certainly no machine gun.

So when this baby bird chirp came out, Brett and I looked at each other in disbelief. At that moment my mother shot us the "keep your mouth closed or else" look. I started to giggle. Brett started to giggle. Mom was turning red and was sending a laser beam of hatred towards both of us with her eyes.

"What is so funny?" Dr. Hartong asked while finishing the last couple bits of his steak.

"It is funny that you should ask that," I replied through my giggles.

"Nothing." My mom tried to interject hoping that she could put out this forest fire that was about to be set ablaze.

"Dr. Hartong…" I responded.

"Call me Mike," he requested.

"Well, Mike, you see that little sneeze that my Mom just let out just took me by surprise. That is all." I explained just waiting to pounce.

"How is that?" he innocently questioned.

"Well, because Mike, when my mother really sneezes it usually sounds like this," Brett added. And the two of us went into the Kathy imitations that our family had done for years. As we reenacted the motions and sounds, we gave Mike the breakdown of the 'build-up phase' to the 'explosion phase.' While my brother and I animated the whole sequence my mother went from red-faced protest, to laughter, to mouth tight just shaking her head and taking the medicine.

The four of us sat around the counter and laughed the night away after that. I remember looking over the table and seeing my mother looking at me and my brother with this sense of pride. An expression that, unfortunately, was sparse due to our crazy existence. She didn't do much talking; she just let Brett and me go on and on telling stories, making Mike laugh.

Funny thing about that night. The Machine Gun Sneeze was never heard again. Mike and my mother got married a little over a year later and have been married for over 25 years. We have tried to coax the 'real' sneeze from my mother ever since. Maybe she won't do it or just can't. Maybe it's lost in a different time and a different place. We will joke that Mike will never know her unless she does the real sneeze, but maybe that is the point. Maybe that along with so many memories from the past, some things were meant to stay behind.

So 'bless you' means something entirely different for this family.

BRETT
Game Winner

My Sophomore year in high school I was trying to make the varsity team in football. I would get some playing time at defensive back, but the time was limited. Some of my most memorable times on the football field were just before the start of practice. My teammates and I would play catch, run joke plays, or try to kick field goals. For the most part the horsing around was our way of unwinding from a day of being in class, sitting in those tiny desks and getting loose before the coaches blew the whistle for organized practice to begin. I was not the kicker, but I had a friend on the team, Jack, who was. He would show me some technique, and I was getting good at blasting the ball through the uprights at close range.

"Damn, Brett you have a strong leg." Jack would say. His encouragement each day gave me the drive to kick a few balls as a routine before practice started. Jack and I would create little competitions where we would bet on who would make the most goals out of five kicks. It was fun to talk trash with Jack and informally compete against each other.

One Friday night our high school was battling with rival Gardner High. Mimi's house on Princeton Street was in Gardner. They were called Chair City because furniture making was a big tradition there. One of the schools near Mimi's house had a huge wooden chair sculpture that we would climb on as kids.

The game was scoreless the first three quarters. Early in the game Gardner kept threatening to score, but our defense held. I made a couple strong tackles, but our team was doing everything to hold this rugged team from breaking the game wide open. They had a very powerful offense. Gardner had a strapping running back who was hard to bring down and a couple good receivers. I got in on some of the plays and was feeling really satisfied with my defense. I could feel the coaches gaining more confidence in me as the game wore on because I was making stops. However, the game was still scoreless going into the fourth quarter, and steady rain soaked the field.

As the field became flat-out sloppy, moving the ball became extremely difficult. Our running back was slipping all over the place. In fact, Jack, who not only kicked field goals but also ran the ball, wrenched his knee on a play pretty bad. He was not able to go back on the field. Although he wasn't our premier running back, it still sucked that he was stuck on the bench.

The fourth quarter was winding down, and we had the ball. We threw once and got a good chunk of yards, but when we tried to throw again, it almost got intercepted. So our coach went to Damien, our strongest running back, and he slogged for a few more yards.

"Brett, come here!" my coach shouted through the rain.

I ran over. "Yes, coach?"

"How are you feeling?"

"Great coach!" I responded. I was having a good game and was really excited but had no idea why he called me over. He never called me over.

"Are you paying attention to this game?" Coach asked.

"Yeah, coach."

"What do you notice?" He questioned.

"That no one can score?" I guessed.

"That is right. Time is running out, and we need to score to win this damn game. We can barely move the ball in this mud bath, and Jack screwed up his knee. Do you know what that means?"

"Not really coach." I was not following his logic at all.

"We need someone to try to kick a field goal."

I did not respond. I squinted through the rain and noticed we were about forty yards out, and Damien was going to run it at least one more time.

"Brett, you think you can make this field goal?" He had his hands on my face mask, and unaffected by the rain, he was not blinking.

I had never kicked in a game. I had only messed around with Jack.

"We have no body else. You are our best bet"

"I can try coach." I was not excited like I was before. I was now terrified. I went from making a few plays as a sophomore feeling good about myself to coach asking me to try and win the game as we brought the game clock to four seconds.

"Take a few warm up kicks and go get 'em," he said with a pat on my shoulder. It was almost a shove in the direction I was supposed to go because my legs did not move right away.

Jack gave me a few pointers as I literally took four practice kicks before I had to go out there. As we got into formation, I could hear the rain and the crowd and noticed that they blended into one constant sound. It merely became a buzzing in my ear.

The ball was snapped and the placekicker set the ball in the squishy ground. Just before I swung my leg from thirty yards out, I notice how the ball didn't sit on top of the grass like it usually did when Jack and I screwed around. Tonight with the rain, the tip of the ball sank into a pool of mud. I drove my foot into it merely trying to repeat what we had done in practice.

Honestly, I didn't look right away. I kept my head down for a moment. It felt good. The ball hit the top of my foot as it usually did when I would go through the routine. It was the humming sound that made me bring my head up. The rain stayed consistent, but the crowd got louder. As my chin came up and the white noise became people's voices, I was able to see the ball sail through the back side of the uprights.

"Yeah, Brett!" my teammates screamed.

"You did it!"

I was tackled and piled on by half the team. My body was pressed into the soggy muck. The scene reminded me of the games we would play in the ball field behind Seven Grove Street, with Brady, David, and Ben. Instead of the sweet smell of grass, this time I got a mouthful of mud.

The next day neighbors gave my mom a clipping from the paper with my name and picture. My mom had a darn scrap book filled with clippings of my brother's feats in running. This was my first one ever, and I hoped it wouldn't be the last. As I studied the small article, I sat a little taller with pride.

"Hey, Mom, you going to start a scrapbook for me too?" I asked.

She looked up from the oven as she tended to the chicken she was roasting.

"What is that Brett?"

"I said, are you going to start a scrapbook with clippings like you do for Brady now?" My tone was a bit more pressing due to the lackluster response the first time.

"Of course I will honey."

That was all I need to hear.

BRADY
Gym Class

My Mother and Mike started dating for a period of time. He would come over from an apartment that he had a couple towns over. We were still living on Seven Grove Street and my mom and he decided to send me to a private Catholic school, Notre Dame, after sixth grade. It was like having my world torn apart. I had never spent much time out of our neighborhood, and I was excited to go to middle school with Ben and my friends whom I had known since kindergarten. I had no interest in going to some school in a completely different town thirty miles away with kids I didn't even know.

I put up a fight, but my arguments were futile. Mike and my mom thought our neighborhood school was too rough and had a drug problem. They thought I would get a better education at this fancy private school.

The school was a mile from the hospital where my mom worked, so I took a long bus ride in the morning and then would walk to the office my mom worked at after school. She had me do some jobs around the office like take out the trash, clean the fish tank, and organize files. She gave me money when I completed my jobs, and I walked down the hill to the convenience store and got M&Ms and Funyuns. I looked forward to riding the elevator down to the basement of the hospital and snooping around all the broken-down equipment and discarded office supplies. These excursions around the office building help me to forget that I hated this new school and missed all my neighborhood friends.

However, nothing could mask the fact the school day was not so good. I hated it. Notre Dame was not kind to outsiders. Most of the kids had been in private school since kindergarten and knew each other. I felt like an outcast, and a few of the guys made sure that feeling intensified as the year went on. Tranor, this kid in almost all of my classes, harassed me every day. In academic classes he would say crap to me about every chance he got and maybe throw a shoulder into me as he walked by. During History he sat behind me and flicked my ears or the back of my neck. In English he would whisper that he was going to 'kick my ass.'

But it was Gym class where he went out of his way to really get me: Tranor would check me in floor hockey when I didn't have the puck, blind side me in football when I was miles from the ball, elbow me in the face in basketball when the gym teacher wasn't looking and then act all concerned.

I could not figure out what he had against me.

"What is your problem?" I asked after he threw his shoulder into me in the hallway, and I dropped all of my books.

"I just don't like you," he responded as he stood above me. He made sure to kick the last book across the hall as I struggled to pick everything up.

Tranor was much bigger than I was, and since his antics kept getting worse, my mind would circle with ideas of how to avoid him. I would take a different way to class, show up in the room just before the bell rang so I could sit away from him. However, my avoidance strategies just made things worse. Tranor just continued to hit me harder and seek me out more often.

One crisp fall day when school dismissed, I exited the back door to cross the parking lot like I normally did each day. Usually I slid through the cut in the fence, followed a path through the woods to the main road and walked to the hospital. On this day, as I crossed the parking lot Tranor stepped out from behind a van and blocked my way to the fence.

"What's up Nichols?" he said with a grin.

"Nothing much Tranor," I responded while alarms went off in my head alerted me that the parking lot was empty because all the other kids took the bus or got picked up in the front of the building.

"I waited for you so I can kick your ass," Tranor bragged while taking a step towards me.

"Man, I don't get it. What is your problem? I never did anything to you," I tried to reason with him.

"I told you, I just don't like you."

He finished that sentence with a good hard push that made me stagger back a step.

"Well, I didn't do anything to you so I don't get what your problem is," I said while telling myself to stay calm and think of what I could do to get out of this mess.

"I don't like the way you look. I don't like the way you smell, and I basically don't like anything about you," he said forcefully as he gave me another shove making me teeter backward again. Now my brain was in full motion. I could turn and run, but I had my backpack and he had nothing. I could ditch the backpack and he could never catch me.

"You are a puss," he said followed by a more forceful shove.

"Stop pushing me," I demanded.

"What are you going to do about it?" he sneered.

I tried to walk around him, but he pushed me against a car. It was time to make a choice. I could run or I could strike first. If I struck first I could then bolt with my bag and possibly make it to the fence.

Just as he started to ask me again what I planned to do about it I hit him as hard as I could with a straight right to the face. I put everything I had behind the strike and I didn't have much. I did not wait for a response: I was already heading for the gap in the fence. However, after five strides I realized he had crumpled on the ground and was crying. I turned and stopped in disbelief. I walked over and stood over him.

"What the hell did you do that for?" he whimpered.

"Are you kidding me? You have been tormenting me since the day I came to this stupid school!" I said as I kicked him in the stomach.

"I wasn't going to do anything. I was just messing with you," he moaned.

"Well, you better stop, asshole," I yelled with another kick to accent my point.

I walked away as Tranor continued to whimper and wipe the blood from his nose and lip. Just before I went through the fence, I looked back not fully understanding what had just happened. I walked to the hospital and did my chores as I always did, and by then my hands had stopped shaking, but my smile had not faded. I cleaned a couple of spots of blood off my knuckles and replied 'not much' when my mom asked what was so funny.

As I threw away the office trash in the back dumpster, I replayed the scene with Tranor in my head. I had a little fear that this could start a war between us, however, in the end it never did. He came to school with his fat lip and never bothered me again. In fact, he kind of started kissing my ass. I still hated going to that school and never really fit in, but it didn't matter. We moved by the end of the year anyway, and I ended up going to another stinking school. At least gym class was a whole lot better.

BRETT
Military Academy

G oing into my Junior year of High School I got shipped to Military Academy. I had been in so much trouble in public school from crummy grades and fighting that my Mom and Mike were trying to do something to knock some sense into me. I fought them on making me go to an Academy where I had to wear a uniform leading up to my enrollment. They thought the discipline and the structure would do me good. So we scheduled a visit to see the campus and meet the football coach. After seeing the football field, weight room facilities, and meeting the coaches I thought hey, it was worth a try. I knew that my path wasn't particularly stellar at this point and maybe I could make some positive changes in my life.

Sports were my sole passion, so I attended school early to participate in the football training camp. I was getting focused and playing against the older players of the Military Academy's football team. I thrived playing against the older players; it was similar to when I would play ball at the parks near Seven Grove Street when I was a kid. Some of the guys on the team were on scholarships and post grads. So I would work extremely hard to impress the coaches to get that ever-precious playing time. The idea would creep into my head that maybe by senior year I could be a leader. My brother was the captain of our track and cross country teams when he was in high school for two straight years and I always thought that was cool. The coaches worked after practice with me for an hour daily to help me hone my skill. They put a lot of time into me. I was playing both ways: defensive back and running back.

"Brett, you need to find the hole and keep those knees driving when you take that initial hit." The coaches would pour schemes into my mind, and I would take all these strategies knowing that they were going to make me better. The founder of The Village, Mr. Billick, played running back, and watching his grainy highlight tapes was etched into my memory. I knew that if he saw what I was doing, he would be proud.

"Remember, you have great hands. Just keep your eyes on the ball. Follow it in. Look for the strip when you wrap the receiver up. Use your power."

To this day that was the best team I have ever been on. Many of those kids went on to college earning scholarships. As my production on the field started to increase the coaches would get in my head the importance of my grades and the scores I needed on the SAT. They were willing to make calls to college coaches as I became a major part of the team. I started to become more and more motivated. Football was the realm I wanted to succeed in, and for the first time I felt like I was in a good place and I could make something of myself.

"Brett, you are a good ball player. You need to keep working hard in the classroom to help balance out what you are doing on the field," they would encourage me. I was never more motivated in the classroom than I was at the Military Academy. For the first time in my life I felt like I could really succeed.

We had maybe lost one or two games all year. The last game of the season was coming up, and my girlfriend Tanya was making a special trip down to visit from miles away. The Academy had strict rules for leaving campus. In order to get off campus, I had to enter special visitation papers which allowed me to be excused for a few hours. Tanya's aunt, who was in her early twenties, brought her down with Tanya's friend Amy. The girls were staying at a nearby hotel, and we were going to hang there for a couple hours because I had to check back into the base soon. The expectation was that I report back promptly at 7pm.

The innocent visit that I had planned without any malicious intentions turned into a drunken mess. Tanya and Amy had convinced the aunt to provide us with some hard alcohol. I had never drank the hard stuff before, and since Tanya was trying to plan this "special" get away going into my last game, I went along with the shots she was passing around. They were mixing these fruity drinks that were going down real easy. I was buzzing hard and having a good time when the booze slammed me just as we were about to leave. I was wrecked. When it came time to return for curfew, I could hardly get my uniform on right. The room would spin at times, and deep down I started to realize I was in some trouble.

The girls dropped me off and I stumbled to the booth where cadets had to report back from leave. The officers knew immediately that I was wasted.

"Nichols you are in big trouble. Head straight back to your barracks!"

Needless to say the bottom fell out. I was suspended for the last game. The coaches' forgiveness was out of reach. They were pissed. I felt bad for letting them down and letting the team down. I had to march an hour everyday for the rest of the year. Unfortunately, the coaches' confidence, my academic performance, and my attitude went downhill from there. Marching everyday made it near impossible to play basketball in the winter. Without sports, I started to get bitter and stopped caring about my classes. It was not long after that I started fighting and getting into trouble just as I did in public school. The school year didn't even end, and the Military Academy wanted to kick me out. I made it to the end of the school year on fumes but was not allowed back for my Senior year. My final year of high school I was reluctantly allowed back to my old public school, and within minutes I was back to doing what I always did - looking for the shortcuts that eventually brought me to nowhere.

BRADY
Hole in the Wall

Mike and my mother got married and we lived in this fancy house he had built in a new town fifty minutes away from where we grew up. We lost our old friends and Brett and I fought a lot. We pummeled each other so much that my mother would leave the house and say, "Boys, no fighting. I mean it. NO fighting."

We always had the best intentions and confidently said, "No problem Mom. We won't." Our biggest fights always seemed to start with great intentions and then our tempers would flare.

My mother was at work during one afternoon a few months after we all moved into a brand new house Mike had built. It was overwhelming going from Seven Grove Street to a fancy street in another town, living in a house where everything was new and pristine. I was watching tv minding my own business. My brother was in his room. Looking back, it was actually pretty peaceful for most of the afternoon.

Brett peeked around the corner giggling as he started throwing little pieces of paper at me. My brother always climbed the walls if he didn't have something active to do for any length of time. I could chill or play on my own when we were little, but he always needed some interaction with others. This day I was not in the mood. As he kept pegging me with pieces of balled-up paper, I gave him a warning.

"Brett, stop it. I am warning you," I grumbled.

Like a moth to a flame my mumbled warning attracted him more. Instead of retreating, he dove on me as I sat on the couch. He quickly put me in a headlock.

"I have you now!" He giggled.

My big-brother status kicked in and I felt that one more mercy warning seemed appropriate.

"Brett man, I am telling you get the hell off me or I am going to kill you."

He tightened up his head lock. "I got YOU man. You will not get out of this one."

I calmly counted to three, which was technically a third warning. If he did not let go, I felt that I had full rights to retaliate by any means necessary.

"1,2,3......" Brett's grip tightened a bit, and he wiggled some to make sure his hold was the best it could be knowing that my counter attack to his ambush was about to start.

I picked him up as he held me in his headlock. I had his legs in my arms and his butt was in the air. I spun him around a couple times to see if he would let go and flee: one more warning essentially. Brett was a fighter, and even though he figured it was about to get uncomfortable, he would rather spar than sit in his room all bored.

And so it was.

After spinning him one last time. I slammed his ass straight and solidly into the wall.

We had not been in our spit shined house for very long with Mike. He and my mother designed it together and it was basically her dream house. It had large exposed beams that stuck out from the drywall. My intention was to ram Brett into a beam, knowing that would make him let go in a hurry. The combination of looking over his backside and him wiggling made my aim off target. When I slammed him as hard as I could into the wall, I had missed the beam.

"Aaaagh, man." he groaned as he immediately let go.

"That will teach you!" I exclaimed as I spun and walked away without even bothering to pay any more attention to him.

Then he moaned, "Help. You gotta get me out of here."

I turned around to figure out what he was moaning about. I missed the beam and put his butt right through the drywall instead. His ass was actually stuck. Brett's feet were off the ground and his hind end was inserted right through the wall.

"Crap." I ran over to his wiggling legs, grabbed his arms and helped pull him out of the wall.

As the two of us stood in front of the damage, the gravity of the situation hit us. We had not been in this new house for more than a freaking week. It was brand new. Our mother left the house saying, 'No fighting." As we looked at each other, we knew this was bad.

"Let's put a picture over it," Brett suggested.

"You're an idiot," I quickly responded. "It would sit on the wall way too low."

As I grew into a young man, I always felt I was able to keep a level head during crisis situations. So many experiences had helped me hone that skill, and here was another. My mother would hit the roof when she saw the gaping hole.

"We have to tell mom at work so she can cool out a bit before she actually sees it," I explained to my brother. This is one of the times where being the older brother sucked because it was already understood that the "lucky" bearer of bad news would be me.

Those movies where you see someone with his head down walking to the gallows, arms tied behind his back as the doom and gloom music whistled in the background - I felt like that. I slowly marched over to the phone in my mother's room with Brett in tow.

"What are you going to say?" Brett asked.

I shrugged as I dialed the phone.

The secretary answered, "Dr. Hartong's office, Nancy speaking...."

"Is Kathy there?" Nancy knew our voices. We called my mother at work a lot.

"Yes, hold on a moment please."

"What is it? I am busy," Mom answered dryly. This was not going to go over very well.

"Mom? Brett and I were messing around and put a hole in the wall. It was a total accident. We can fix it. It was an accident, really."

"What? Brady, quit messing around. I don't have time."

"No Mom. I am serious. We put a hole in the wall upstairs on accident."

"Goddamn you two! Are you serious? Both of you are to go to your rooms and not come out until I get home." Her words came through the phone at rapid-fire pace.

"OK Mom. We will. Sorry. We can fix it."

"You heard me." The phone went dead. She slammed that thing down, and we knew we were toast.

Mom eventually came home. She saw the hole. She screamed at us. Funny thing was that when she told us to get to our rooms on the phone, we were so scared that we actually sat in our rooms for two hours until she came home. We could have tip toed out, but we didn't. We could have watched tv until we heard the garage door open and then run back to our rooms. Nope. We actually went to our rooms. If anything, we talked a little bit through the wall asking each other what we thought she might do to us.

After screaming at us and telling us what 'barbarians' we were, she sent us back to our rooms. "Just wait until Mike comes home."

This was an interesting phase in our life. Mike was not our real father. My mother and he had a little wedding somewhere after a period of dating, and my brother and I were not even there to see her married. I guess it had something to do with the 'barbarian' thing. Anyway, she seemed intent on injecting him into this problem.

When Mike came home, I heard her giving him the blow-by-blow through my door. Minutes later there was a light tap on my door.

"Brady, open up."

I opened the door and laid back on my bed, keeping my distance, not knowing how this was going to go.

With his hand behind his back holding something, he asked me what happened.

I told him, and as I did I noticed he was holding his fraternity paddle: this large wooden chunk of wood that had three Greek symbols etched into the surface. I had been in this situation before with a large man holding a piece of wood about to hit me with it. Thoughts of escape flooded my mind.

Meanwhile downstairs my mother hollered like crazy.

"Michael you have to teach these boys a lesson!"

"They are barbarians!"

"They need to be taught respect!"

I did not see the same darkness in his eyes as in the Old Man's. I yelled past him, "Mom, seriously, we are blood!"

I then focused back on Mike.

"You aren't going to hit me with that thing are you?"

"No," he sighed. "Of course not. Your mother is just really upset."

He closed the door and sat on my bed.

I don't know if he even went into Brett's room to have the same conversation. Sometimes with things like this, the information that one of us got was just automatically assumed to be relayed to the other. Nevertheless, Mike and I actually had a conversation. A conversation about our mess up, about us fixing it and paying for the hole. It was the first time in my life that the man holding the stick chose not to use it.

BRETT
Man in the Mirror

My senior year I was lucky to graduate. Looking back, I can't believe that I did. While my brother was away at college, my life with Mom and Mike became strained. One cold February afternoon my parents left for the weekend. I started dipping into the case of Coors Light my step-dad kept in the garage. After a few and a good buzz, I called this girl, Cindy, I was seeing on and off and invited her over.

She and I were hanging out and drinking together, making calls to figure out where the parties were later on that night. We were plastered. It was getting dark, and it was getting cold. Seeing some headlights flash past the bedroom window made me look outside and notice a vehicle had pulled in our driveway.

"Stay here," I told Cindy. I staggered out of the bedroom shirtless and barefoot. I opened the front door and just looked at this SUV that I didn't recognize, sitting in our driveway.

"What the hell," I muttered to myself. "Cindy stay upstairs," I ordered her before I foolishly walked out in the winter air half-dressed and shoeless.

The SUV was not moving, nor was anyone stepping out of it, so I walked right up to the window, cupped my hands and peered into it. I did not recognize the driver or the passenger so I just assumed they just had the wrong address. I shrugged them off and started to make my way back to the house.

"Look at this crazy white boy; he got no clothes on." As I turned toward the familiar voice I got cracked in the head. As I stumbled back, I recognized the guy who hit me. This guy, Victor, had smoke with me because his girl was giving me attention at school. He was too much of a coward to come at me alone so he brought a few of his friends, whom I didn't know. They started to surround me in my own damn yard.

"That is all you got you fuckin' pussy?" I said as I blasted Victor right in the face. The other guys paused after my first assault, probably contemplating what the half-dressed crazy kid was going to do next. Conflicts that I got into usually would happen for me this way: a switch would go in my head and my mind would say, 'screw it.' Then I would attack. I threw everything I had at him and was soon on him, pounding the crap out of his face. Bad move on my part. Focusing on him, I was left exposed, and the other guys took advantage. They immediately jumped me. Multiple boots, a bat, and fists rained down on my head and body. I covered my head the best I could, but the blows kept coming until I don't remember them coming any longer.

I do remember just seeing the blurry SUV's taillights disappear. I somehow made my way to the door shivering. Cindy was in tears after watching the whole brawl from my bedroom window.

"Oh, my God Brett, your face," she said in horror.

I was numb from the beating or the cold. My head was throbbing, and I didn't exactly know where the pain was coming from. After looking at myself in the mirror I understood why Cindy was hysterical. I looked worse than Rocky after Clubber Lang pulverized him. One eye was completely closed. One half of my jaw was deformed. Later we went to the hospital to find out my jaw and ribs were broken. When my mother and Mike came home and saw my face, realized the beer was gone, and I professed that I would seek revenge on the dudes who did this to me, my mom was horrified.

"Brett, listen to yourself," she pleaded. She squinted her eyes as if she didn't know to whom she was talking.

A growing sense loathing or doubt flooded my mother's expression. Now I realized how disfigured my face was from the beating. The battered and bruised face was not mine any longer. When I gently ran my fingertips across the jagged contour nothing registered. This event was the last straw: my mother and Mike kicked me out of the house. I was forced to stay with friends for the rest of my senior year. I bounced around from house to house. I often had memories of that swollen and bruised face in the mirror exposing a person who was becoming less and less recognizable.

BRADY
First Race

By the time I got to High School, I had bounced from school to school and started to feel pretty isolated. Back when I was real young I always had my neighborhood friend Gavin. Coming into my new Public High School I basically knew no one. I was never a kid who had a bunch of friends, but I usually had at least one or two that I could really count on. Now I knew not a soul.

My Mom and new step dad Mike wanted me to do a sport. I had never done an organized sport because I sucked at everything. But a kid in English class asked me to come out for Cross Country.

"They will take anyone," he said. He went on to say that he had noticed in gym class that we battled with all the running stuff, and I was pretty fast so I should give it a shot. I agreed only because he put me on the spot, but I really had no intention of showing up to practice.

I went home that night and told my Mom that this kid in English class wanted me to go out for Cross Country.

"That is a great idea. You should do that," my mom said in a hopeful-laced-with-a-crap-ton of skepticism tone knowing that I never did squat all through Middle School, including all the times when she even tried to force me.

"Yeah, maybe," I said.

By the time this kid finally got me to agree, it was towards the end of the week. I did not even know what Cross Country was. I just knew you ran and I was kinda fast. Well, I showed up to practice the day before a meet. A meet, I found out that day, is what they call the race against other schools. So the coach told us to go run 30 minutes total. He told us to run out about fifteen minutes and turn around and come back. I noticed that everyone had these cool running shoes. I just had these tennis type shoes that I wore everywhere. They were comfortable because I wore them all the time. But a ton of the guys were saying that I had to get some running shoes like they had. At this point buying a new pair of shoes seemed like way too much effort. There was a big chunk of me that felt like I might not be doing this tomorrow so I was not going to be worrying about shoes.

Anyway, the coach put me with a group of freshmen and some sophomores. We started on our run, and as soon as we rounded the corner by this cemetery, all the guys stopped. We all walked into the graveyard where there was a water fountain. The guys just sat around and sprayed water at each other. They sat on the grass and leaned on the tombstones and messed around. I was pretty surprised. I mean I thought the workout was going to be hard, and it was turning out to be really easy. We just screwed off until one of the Sophomores said, "ok. It is time to start heading back."

We showed up to the practice field right around 30 minutes later just like the Coach wanted us to do. The guys giggled and acted all tired. The Coach asked them how it went.

"Great Coach! Getting ready for the meet tomorrow," they said so convincingly.

"Awesome, this is going to be a challenging race. St. Bernard's has a strong team."

Coach never asked me how I felt. He didn't say one word to me until we were about to end practice.

"We have a meet tomorrow. Here is your uniform," he stated. There was this long awkward pause as I processed what he was in-directly implying.

"You want me to race?"

"Yeah, why not?"

"I don't know," but inside I was thinking: how am I supposed to do this? I don't know where to go. What to do. Pure terror started to set in. Are you kidding me?

"You just jump in the race and follow the rest of the guys," he went on like it was the best idea ever. "Just have fun with it."

Considering that he was telling me and not asking me, I just said, "OK."

This was one of those times that being such a chicken bit me in the ass. I was silent instead of saying, "Hell, no, I only just ran today," or "Are you crazy, I am not even sure I want to do this after today."

I could have maybe even tried to be all mature like my mom wanted me to be and said, "Coach, that is a great idea, however, don't you think we are kind of jumping into things a little fast? I mean today was my first day remember?"

Nope. Instead I just stood there like a dumb ass.

When my Mom picked me up from that first day of practice I was ready to break down.

"How did it go?" she asked.

"Horrible. I mean easy, but he wants me to race tomorrow." I had to just try and stay calm. I had this fleeting hope that she might come to my aid and maybe see that I was by no means ready to race some race on some course in some sport that I knew noth-ing about.

"Oh, that sounds like it would be good for you."

So the following day after school on my second day of Cross country and my second day of even knowing what this sport was about, I prepared for my first race. I just followed all the other JV guys around. When they jogged, I jogged. When they stretched, I stretched. And of course when the gun went off, and they started to run, so did I. As all these runners took off from the line I just looked for the kid who invited me to come out in the first place. I ran next to him for a while. It didn't take long for the pack to kind of settle down and start to spread out. The boy in my English class who had convinced me to come out started breathing heavy. He turned to me just before the half-way point of the race and said, "Man, you look good. Move up!"

"Ok."

Really I didn't feel that bad at that moment. So I started pushing a little harder. I slowly passed other runners making my way up toward the front. I finally reached the two leaders from the other school. I just stayed behind them. First off, I didn't know where the heck I was going. Second, I was not convinced I could keep this up. As we got closer to the end of the race, one guy faded and fell back, and it was just me and the runner from St. Bernards. As we rounded the final bend, the varsity guys and the spectators started to cheer. Guys from our team were jumping up and down and screaming because they could not believe I was up toward the front. Until that last turn I still was never certain of where I was supposed to go and by then the pace had really gotten faster. Once I saw the finish line I burst into an all-out sprint. I was stunned that the other runner could not respond. He just let me go. My lungs were on fire. My legs were heavy as heck, but as soon as I got a few steps on him and could see the finish before me, all that discomfort took a back seat to a feeling of exhilaration. Part of it was all the people cheering my name and going crazy. However, the bigger part was that I literally sucked at everything. Especially athletics. This was the first time that I succeeded at something. Not to mention I actually won. I won. I could not believe it.

As guys started to cross the line behind me and the rest of the competitors finished the race, the coach was going around asking if I had gotten lost or mistakenly cut the course. He soon found out that I stayed with the field and won straight up.

"That was a great effort, Brady," Coach said with a questioning tone.

"Thanks Coach," I was smiling from ear to ear.

The whole ride home I gave my mother the blow-by-blow account of the race. She didn't even seem that surprised. It was as if she expected it.

She just calmly responded, "I knew it would be good for you."

Good for me was an understatement. It changed everything. People in the hallway knew who I was. They said my name on the announcements. I never ran JV again but ran Varsity from that day forward. I climbed up to the second runner on the team before the season was over. Me being good at Cross Country opened up a countless connections I never had. Teachers were nicer and asked me how races were. Kids were cooler and didn't seem to look at me like I had two heads. Girls talked to me and asked me out.

The more I raced the better I got at it. The better I got at it the more attention I received. I soon discovered I might not be the coward that I always thought I was. I was actually pretty tough. The endeavor that is running is really about taking discomfort or straight-up pain. I could do that. I didn't approach it as who was the fastest; I approached it as who would outlast the other person. Other kids looked at their watch or measured the distance. I just looked at it as beating the guy next to me. Growing up I felt like I was always getting beaten down. It felt great being the guy who could do the beating for once.

BRETT
College Experience

A fter getting kicked out of Military Academy, I went back to my public high school to finish out my senior year. My sport dreams were shattered, I was not motivated to do well in high school, and hanging out with the wrong guys became my favorite pastime. I became that guy who was looking for the best party and shunned all the responsibilities I once held dear. I was already moving house to house because mom and Mike wouldn't have me after the big fight in the front lawn.

While hanging around on Highland Avenue with Todd and some older guys, we found out about a college party that was going down that night at the local university the next town over. College parties were the best for guys like me who were losing their identity in high school. I was looking for new and risky experiences. Sometimes I thought that if I wasn't able to attend college as a student, I could at least go to the parties. If something was about to jump off, I wanted to be in the thick of it and get my 'college experience' that way.

I was so excited to see what would happen at every party that if nothing was going on I made sure to inject some action.

When Todd and my crew got to this one particular college blowout, we wanted to get in the mix and not stand out right away. There were clear differences in the way that we dressed versus these college dudes. However, I didn't care about how we looked; inside I was simmering, just waiting for the opportunity to explode.

Todd was hitting on a college girl, and an age-old conflict ensued: boy-meets girl-who-is-committed-to-another then boys-lock-horns-in-battle-over-girl. Todd and the girl began with a little small-talk, and her over protective boyfriend soon got agitated. Hastily, I made my way to intervene.

"You got a problem with my friend?" I defiantly asked.

"Who the fuck are you?" he responded, with his chest pushed out. He sized me up, and recognized immediately from the grunge look of our crew that I was not a college student. He most likely underestimated me as well.

"Let's go outside, and I will introduce myself you pussy!" I shouted, prompting him to accept my invitation.

We went outside, and everyone sensing the drama streamed out after us. The crowd formed a loose circle in anticipation of some form of confrontation. He began to talk tough, trying to intimidate me. This guy did not realize that I did not go outside to talk. I did not fret if I won or lost. In mid-sentence, I cracked him in the jaw. As he staggered back, I stayed on him and kept the blows raining down on his face. After he went down, I beat the brakes off of him.

His buddies tried to jump on me, and it soon became mayhem. Some of my boys were tangled with some of his. Bodies slammed into cars, dropped in the street, and some ran away. It didn't take long for The Wagon to come.

"Let's get out of here!" someone yelled. That felt like an alarm going off. Dudes started to scatter like cockroaches when the cop lights exploded. I cut through back yards, jumped some fences and eventually got away.

One of the college guys got seriously hurt, and his parents wanted to sue someone. Within days the authorities were bearing down on those involved, putting the pieces together.

"I didn't see nothing," was my response when the cops got to me. But the pressure of the authorities got to some of the boys, and soon it was out that I was the first to throw a punch. That was my first criminal charge: Assault and Battery. The parents of the injured kid wanted to sue my parents. I wasn't even living at home. Between bouncing from house to house, court proceedings and conferences, I began my first dance with the legal system. This 'College Experience' drove a huge wedge between me and my parents and marked the beginning of my "education" path of a different sort.

BRADY
Under the Bridge

After changing schools three or four times, I finally settled in Lunenburg. It was a small town about thirty-five miles from Grove Street. After a few years of going to high school in our new town and living in the house that Mike had built for our mother, I started to feel like life was normal. I never stopped writing to my friend Gavin when we moved. He and I would always promise each other that we were going to visit. Finally one weekend we set a date: I was going to drive back and visit him and his family. Four years had passed, and I was excited to go back to my old stomping grounds and see his family. There was a stint growing up where I slept over at his house almost every weekend. His was like a second family to me.

The weekend was nothing short of surreal. Gavin wasted no time taking me to the Three Pipes, the dam where we would pull sucker fish out of the murky water with our bare hands, and the abandoned factory where we would climb on the roof and jump off into snow banks during big winter storms. We paid a surprise visit to Charlie who was pregnant now and had stopped going to high school. She made light of how she struggled getting up steps compared to the last time I saw her where she was smacking homeruns over the fences in Little League.

The last afternoon that Gavin and I were together we reminisced about the old days while standing on the stone bridge on Elm:

Roaming all over the neighborhood, we would spend some days by the Three Pipes or the Quarter Mile. Other days we would head down to the river and climbed all over the Dam or swung on the footbridge that scaled across the murky river. Apparently, some paper mill polluted the river, and that is why the thick water was muddy brown and smelled really bad. It looked like a river of chocolate, like in that Willie Wonka movie. When we fished out of it, we were not allowed to eat the fish. Of course, you would have to be the biggest imbecile to eat anything near the river because the smell alone screamed it was toxic. Besides, all anyone could get out of it was sucker fish or small horned-pout. We caught the sucker fish by hand where they congregated in the still water. Gavin and I built forts behind his house and sometimes went into town to buy candy from the convenience store. We didn't venture there much, but when we did we sometimes went under the big stone bridge where Elm Street turned to Maple Street. Downtown was north of the river, and our neighborhood was on the south side. If you jumped over the road barriers and scaled down the embankment, you could get under the bridge and sit on the large rocks and watch the water flow by as the traffic above thumped along.

The mammoth rocks that lined the underside of the bridge held all kinds of treasures. We found fishing tackle, various bottles, and mostly porn. Homeless guys slept down there in the warmer weather, so quite a collection of junk accumulated. Gavin and I prowled around looking for loot. I found a fishing pole once that worked perfectly. The porn was all ripped up, but Gavin and I pointed at the pictures and giggled because we were little, and the women had huge breasts and were in funny poses.

While it was adventurous to drop down under the bridge to catch a couple glances of naked women in magazines or rummage through trinkets, we had to be careful in the summer because more homeless guys would be active down there. They were pretty territorial and scary as hell.

One summer afternoon while Gavin and I rummaged around, we found a little tarp set up as a tent with a bunch of stuff under it. Our hearts raced, knowing that the dude who owned it surely wasn't far away.

"Look at this stuff," Gavin said as he pulled out some cigar boxes of pictures and a couple of pocket knives from under the makeshift tent. We found not only ripped-up nude pictures, but also fully-intact magazines. We giggled like crazy. But just when we were about to bust into looking at one of the forbidden books, we heard a gravelly voice shout at us.

"Hey, what the hell are you two doing?"

We turned to see a bearded and dirty skeleton of a man scaling the rocks toward us. He looked so disheveled under the darkness of the bridge that at first he didn't look human. We were not sure if he came from above the bridge like we had or had crawled out of the darn river! Regardless, we dropped everything and sprinted toward the opposite side of the bridge and scurried up to the street. The granite rocks under the bridge were big and sharp, but I am pretty sure that in our state of panic, Gavin and I prang lightly and tip-toed across them like ninja warriors. As the Loch Ness Monster of a guy fumbled his way towards his hideout to see if we had stolen anything, Gavin and I were gone. I don't think I ever moved that fast. We used our hands and feet to scale the dirt path up to the surface of the bridge to the safety of humanity. Just seeing the sunlight and cars going by gave us a bit of comfort.

However, our fear still lingered, so we sprinted down Maple and did not let up until we got to Gavin's street.

By that time we were panting and laughing all at once. Being so young and seeing that guy come out of nowhere made us sprint the length of town and not stop until we were well away from the bridge. As we sat on Gavin's stoop, we realized we left our bikes down by the river. We always stashed them out of sight in the bushes. After a little "pros and cons" discussion, we decided that one run-in with the Loch Ness Guy was plenty for one day and planned to go back the next day and get our bikes to start another adventure all over again.

Though my life with Mom and Mike was more stable than the old days when refuge with Gavin provided temporary reprieve from the Old Man, laughing with my childhood friend that weekend helped me to gain perspective of where I had come from and where I wanted to go.

BRETT
Reflection

My brother was off in college, and some of my friends were starting their first year at a university, in the military, or going to work. I was left behind as my old crew was stepping into other worlds, leaving behind our small Massachusetts town. I perceived that I had already cashed all my chips and still was stuck here. I reflected on the dreams of playing ball in college and owning a business, but those were starting to fade. My consistent school troubles solidified the feeling that those goals were miles and miles behind me now.

Todd and a few of my friends who stuck around town were out driving around in my beat- up Escort with the ripped up vinyl seats and the cracked driver's side window. NWA blared on the car stereo. A couple of the guys had cocaine on them. Coke was starting to get big in some parts of the neighborhood. The guys starting passing it around as we sat idle in an abandoned parking lot. I had gotten into many fights, been kicked out of school and caught for drinking, but up until this day, I never did drugs. There was bleakness associated with drug use that signaled the user had given up, that those who used had cashed in on those dreams and bought the high that they would ride for that moment. While I had the mirror in one hand and a straw in the other I always thought that maybe my time had passed as well. One year ago I thought I would be doing something else that was big with my life: maybe scoring the winning touchdown in a college game or working toward my own business. However, as my opportunities started to dwindle, I was committed to get that feeling of scoring that touchdown back.

I looked past the powder on the mirror and saw my face. It occurred to me that I would normally look in the mirror to comb my hair, brush my teeth, and to check out how I looked. I normally used the reflection to take care of myself. This time I stared into the mirror, and looking back was a young man who was about to do the forbidden. Little did I know that there was no going back. I lowered my head in defeat in order to sniff the coke off the glass. With my chin to my chest, I heard voices from my past saying, "Don't be a loser. Pick your head up. Don't be a loser." I ignored these voices. I let the high kick in. Once the drip came and travelled through my body, everything changed. Everyone became a friend, every situation seemed manageable, and my surroundings became bigger and better. My beat-up Escort felt like the Ritz, the lights and sound were so intense. The dreams that felt like miles away before didn't bother me at all anymore. Those worries became the dust I was breathing up my nose and helped me feel as if I were in a better place.

Minutes later all four of us were chopping lines while selling new dreams to one another. I was so high that I never wanted the night to end. We cruised from house party to house party. Being around people just intensified the high, and that was all I wanted for now. Night melted into day and then to night again. Evening stumbled and got lost to the next morning. The first time I got high I stayed up for three days straight.

That first night I touched coke was the beginning of a relation-ship; the drugs became a girl I would date for many years. She touched me, and I was unable to let her go. So many times I tried to break up with her. I wanted to leave her so many times. But her grip just restrained me and became tighter and tighter. Somewhere along the way I think I stopped fighting. I just couldn't seem to get away. The beginning of my drug use was the euphoric stage of the intimate relationship where everything seems heightened. The early days made me feel free, but as the affair went on I started to realize I was trapped. Each time I used I was flooded with this mixture of release followed by a deep hatred of myself. Eventually I started to sink slowly, and as time wore on, I began descending faster. Just as the time my face was disfigured from getting my face beat by those cowards outside my house, it became harder and harder to recognize my reflection in the mirror. Except now I was deformed in another way.

BRADY
Batman

Mary and I dated for close to a year in high school. She and I hung out with her older sister, Trish, and Trish's boyfriend, Donny, sometimes. Going to Mary's house and hanging with her parents and Trish's sister was fun. They all seemed so close. Some nights we played board games, watched movies, or went out. One evening when her parents were out, we had a 'couples night' over a vicious game of Monopoly with Trish and Donny. In the middle of the game Mary ran down in the basement to change the laundry quickly. A few minutes later she came screaming upstairs with an empty laundry basket.

"There is a bat down there!"

"Oh, my god, it flew right at my head!"

Her sister and I consoled her so she could get the rest of the details out. Once she was calm, Donny and I decided to be valiant and take care of the situation. I grabbed the fire poker, and he snatched a tennis racquet, and we made our way to the basement. It took us a while to find the light switch; as soon as we did the bat started to flit around. A couple times it cruised right by my head and I lashed out with the fire poker. Donny and I were striking out each time the bat dive bombed our heads.

"Give me the tennis racquet," I said after noticing he wasn't even coming close to hitting the vermin. With the wider weapon I felt confident I could get it.

"Dang!" Donny yelled as one pass the bat made was really close to his head.

Eventually, after the bat made a few more back and forth passes, I connected.

"Awwww!" Donny and I exclaimed in unison as the racquet mashed the bat in mid flight.

"Brady got it!" Donny celebrated as he ran up the stairs.

I scooped the bat up with the racquet and exited out the cellar door. Apparently, this opened up to the back of the house. Being close to midnight, it was pitch black outside. I was a bit disoriented with the darkness and had never been in Mary's back yard before. I walked several paces straight back until I hit some taller bushes. I figured this was the edge of their lawn and I had now reached the tree line. I took the heel of my boots and dug into the soft soil a few times, making a shallow hole. After dropping the carcass in, I kicked some soil back over the shallow grave and headed back inside.

"Problem solved," I stated confidently as everyone giggled at our re-enactment of the battle down in the basement.

In typical Monopoly fashion, the game went on too long, and we all lost interest. When the night ended and I was about to leave, Mary reminded me that tomorrow we were going to the park with some friends.

"I will pick you up around noon," I reaffirmed.

That next day I came over and was greeted by Mary's stepfather, Pete. He was a really cool guy who was always joking around. He had this great menu collection. For each menu he hijacked, there was story of how he got it without capture. The leather-bound ones from fancy restaurants always had the most elaborate stories. He had instances where he put them in the liner of his coat, or he had to get Mary's mom distract the waiter as he went back to his car to get something. Pete always had tricks and jokes he would tell me about.

"Hey, Brady, have you ever seen my gardens?" Pete asked.

"No," I replied, wondering why he would ask me this now.

"It will take Mary a few more minutes to get ready. Let me show you," he insisted.

Wanting to make a good impression on the parents of my then-girlfriend, I figured "why not?" I shrugged and he led me out the front door and around the back.

"I am particularly proud of my peas," he said.

"They grow real tall and wrap around these wooden stakes I pound in the ground," Pete continued.

I wasn't that interested in gardening, but he seemed pretty excited. So I nodded and looked real engaged.

"Cool," I said with the most enthusiastic tone I could muster.

"Check this out," he said as he gestured towards this lush garden in front of us.

That is when it hit me. It wasn't as if someone tapped me on the shoulder and said, "Now do you get it?" or a light bulb flicked on above my head. It was like a boulder being dropped from the sky on the Wile E. Coyote.

As he pointed to the garden, I first noticed some boot prints in the rich dirt. The deep footprints stomped through a full row of peas to end right in the middle of the garden. Trampled peas and stakes were flattened in a small clearing, obviously made by the massacre of the boots. Then I saw a very shallow grave with a pathetic bat wing sticking out of it.

"I am so sorry," I apologized. I was mortified after surveying the scene for what it was. At night I envisioned myself digging a grave at the edge of the yard not plowing through my girlfriend's father's garden.

"I couldn't see back here and...."

"Don't worry about it," he interrupted my developing excuse in the most gracious manner. "Hey you were saving my two daughters from this creature," he said with more than a hint of sarcasm.

"Do you want me to fix it?" I asked.

"Oh, no. I will take care of it from here," Pete said as he put his arm around me and led me back to the house.

"You did enough for one day, Batman," he said with a smile.

BRETT
The Job

Sequestered were the memories of football and pole vaulting, the training village, and my athletic dreams. Lately I did not care much if I lived or died. My mind was made up.

Yet I remembered the feeling of being sandwiched in the middle of the game of pickle we would play in the old ball park.

"I am going to get you Brett!" they would say.

Back and forth the players would toss the ball and try to lull me to lose focus.

Some would wait for the defense to make the first move, to take a shot first as they stalked the runner. Not me. I always would get on base because I struck first.

I grabbed my backpack stocked with my mask, gloves, hammer with plenty of rounds, and a full change of clothes. I pushed the contradictory thoughts that leaked into my mind deeper into the fog. It was rainy and visibility was low like those aspirations that were so far away. I loaded the dirtbike into the back of the pick up truck and tore off to the drop spot, secluded in the woods where my crew had roamed as little kids, and only we knew the trails like the back of our hands. I had scoped this area out for months.

Deep into the forest was still with only small critters skitting around cracking the silence. As I was getting my dirt bike off the bed of the truck, I envisioned Ben, Kevin, Brian, and Brady with me dodging through the trees laughing and jumping. I refocused my efforts on the gamble that I was about to make: that like in pickle I was going to beat the defense. I suited up, put the back-pack on, then kicked the bike over, cranking the engine and listening to the whine split the forest calm.

As I ripped through the woods on my motorcycle, my adrenaline was pumping harder than any tackle I ever made. My emotions went from zero to one hundred and remained pinned on the red line. I got a sick feeling that grew stronger and stronger as I got closer to where I would leave the bike. Like in the weight room pushing myself during a major workout, muscles ached and a sick bile taste lingered in the back of my mouth. I was ready to puke once I cut the engine. However, I waited under the cover of some shrubs by the road until I gathered myself.

When there was a lull in traffic I stepped into the light knowing there was no turning back now. I moved swiftly towards the bank, head down, moving fast but not so fast as to draw attention. I hit the door and pulled the mask down all in one movement. The hammer was out and pointing at the teller.

"Give me the money in the drawer!" I demanded. I knew they kept the big bills under the drawer. With the hammer staring them down I went to each teller. The safe was locked, but I was able to hit the drive-through deposit. I stuffed the bag with cash as quickly as I could while heading out the door. I scanned the road as I scoured the surroundings as if coming out of Clem's Diner. When I got back to the patch of woods and kicked the bike to life, a trickle of relief flowed through me as I ripped down the trails. My heart continued to pound as I hustled to the changing point.

Fifteen minutes and I was there; I could already hear the whine of the sirens off in the distance. I was certain no one saw me come out of the bank - I was a ghost. The commotion of the cruisers was racing to the scene, but I was long gone. I smoked a cigarette to calm my nerves while I changed my clothes and buried the bag of money and gear. I did not even know how much was in the bag. I would worry about that at a later time. This was about executing the job.

When I was back with the bike loaded in truck, I immediately put distance between the money, gear, and me. The goal now was to get far away from the treasure. My stash was buried in the dirt that our little feet had trampled so many years back. Our worn-out sneakers, our giggles, our smiles were left out in those woods along with the spoils that I had just buried. Except this was not on an ancient pirate map that we would follow as a guide as we roamed the woods for hours. Buried in those woods was another demon that would eventually claw its way out of the ground and forever change my life.

BRADY
The Raid

After graduating from High School I ran at Phillips Exeter Academy and then attended Lawrence University. Rhonda and I had married after graduating from UW-Madison with my MFA and had our first child. I was planning to become a teacher, so we were spending the summer at the Training Village working with the new generation of campers. Mr. Billick welcomed me with open arms. The two summers that I had spent at the Village racing those morning runs as a high school kid prepared me for running in college. Now to come back and help new campers was exciting and rewarding. Having Rhonda and our new son, who was barely crawling, experience this unique island of my past life was surreal. I would workout with the campers, counsel them, and meanwhile Rhonda got to bring our son Kye around to watch all the activities. Rhonda was showered with stories of "Brady as a camper."

"No one could ever beat Brady on the morning runs," Mr. Billick would say.

"He was out of the shower and changed before the next runner came in."

As a counselor I was gratified to motivate the young athletes in the runs as I rolled along-side them.

One Saturday afternoon Rhonda, Kye, and I went to visit Mimi. Her house on Princeton Street was just a couple towns over, and it was always fun to get away from camp life for a few hours. We had been visiting Mimi for an hour or so when out of the window we saw two dark figures pass by. We all jumped up, startled by their stealthy gestures moving about the back yard. As soon as we noticed the figures in the back window, we noticed that there were a few in the front as well.

"Open up! This is the police! You are surrounded!"

Their forceful command not only startled us but more importantly really frightened Mimi, so I instinctively went to her side to calm her. Honestly we didn't even know what the figures instructed because they yelled through the door and took us by surprise.

"Brady, what is going on?" she quivered.

"What do they want?"

Mimi's pleas and questions were soon answered as the swat team barrelled in the front door.

"Where is Brett Nichols?" they demanded. They ordered us to the ground, and we immediately complied. Once they realized that we weren't a threat, some went off to different rooms, and a couple stayed in the room with us. They allowed us to get up and sit on the couch. I sat between Mimi and Rhonda as Rhonda held Kye in her lap. The three of us remained erect in our postures still afraid to move. I rubbed Mimi's back and told her it was going to be fine.

"Is Brett Nichols here?" The commander handed me a warrant that I didn't bother to read because I was focused on Mimi's desperate worry.

"Brady, what is going on?" Mimi whispered a few more times. I helplessly responded that they were looking for Brett.

When the swat team realized that we were the only individuals in the house, they allowed us to get up and move around. Rhonda was able to put Kye down and let him play on the floor. Meanwhile, men were ripping through the house looking for something other than just my brother. They were leaving nothing to chance and overturning everything.

"Again, do you have any idea where Brett may be?" The officer closest to us firmly questioned.

"We don't know," I responded in a very irritated manner due to the repetition.

Not only did we not know where Brett was, but we had no idea what this disruption was about, and every attempt to ask was cut off by more questions or silent gestures as they conversed into various radio devices. Meanwhile, we could see men searching outside and inside. Some were even digging through the mulch pile out back.

"What are you looking for?" I asked. The simple question was met with no verbal response but with more radio chatter and more furniture overturned and ripped open.

After what seemed like eternity, the lead person who was not only giving us the most commands but also commanding others around him came over to us.

"Brett has been picked up on the interstate without incident," he stated matter-of-factly. He then added, "We have a warrant to search the premise." They tore into the place. The apartment above Mimi's garage, where Brett had lived for some time, got the most attention and had the most destruction. The group of officers searched every inch of that house. We had no idea what they were looking for, but it was clear they were desperate to find something.

"Sorry for the inconvenience, but we were under the impression that Brett might be at this location armed and dangerous."

As facts started to come to light, we found out that Brett was under arrest for bank robbery. The wave of disbelief hit us all. Brett had done some messed-up stuff, but we had trouble comprehending that person the authorities tore the house up for was my brother.

When the cops left, we walked around Mimi's house like ghosts absorbing the overturned furniture and items. Mimi stared at the home she had lived in for fifty years, and whimpers periodically escaped her lips when she saw some of the most disheveled parts of the house. The scene brought me back to Seven Grove Street where the Old Man had sometimes done the same to our house. Even Mimi's dirt basement where she solely stored art supplies was overturned. The dirt floor where Brett and I would make roads and play with our matchbox cars had large ambitious boot prints trampling in various directions.

Mimi suffered from the ordeal. It wasn't long after the raid that she sold her house and moved with Uncle Phil to Maine. She could not tolerate being in the house any longer. When I asked her why the sudden move she would just state that it was time.

"It just is time to close the book," she would reiterate.

It was clear that she felt violated and probed so intensely that every time she entered her home she would re-live the agonizing experience. The memories of the summers, the artwork on rainy days, and the bustling Christmas parties were all forced to follow us out the door. These reflections now had to exist independently in our minds for years to come. None of us have ever returned to Mimi's house on Princeton Street nor have we discussed the raid.

BRETT
The Kennel

I got eighteen to twenty years for the bank job. The first couple years were the hardest. Days would just bleed into one another while I was locked up. I spent my time trying to figure out how to hustle on the inside. I tried to continue to do what I knew, learning nothing from my mistakes. On one hand I was surrounded by concrete block, and on the other, more distant hand, was my freedom again. My mind thought along the lines of pulling jobs in order to survive the first couple years. Trying to do work in here was more extreme because opportunities did not come along very often. I would attempt to push drugs or other commodities inmates wanted into the joint, but intel over the phone with unreliable men would inevitably lead to the schemes crashing. So as I worked on this eighteen-to-twenty year stint, it became clear that I would have to choose a more honest path.

As time rolled along I began to feel the walls of prison were the end for me. I would never return to my former self. I felt as though I would be locked up forever and this is where my life would end. I constantly reflected on how I failed at every attempt to get ahead. Every day and every night I was stuck in the confines of my room. I would only get out of my cell for one hour Monday through Friday and the cell would get smaller and smaller - the walls would seem to close in on me. I would lose track of the days -- and sometimes the years -- forgetting how long I had been in. Visits dwindled, mail became sparse, and the yard and the gym stopped helping me to pass the time.

I began reading. I would read anything I could get my hands on. Before picking up a book I had been waiting for, I would sometimes laugh at the irony because I had hated to read in school. My teachers could not get me to crack a book. I could not sit still in school, always jumping around and getting up to be a clown, so focusing on an open book was not going to happen. In the joint I even found enjoyment reading four-day-old-out-of-date newspapers. Time moved faster outside these walls and stood still in here, so reading out of date news was just fine with me.

Early in my bid, I didn't come into contact with anyone very often, so unless one of the fellow inmates that I was tight with got put on the same tier, I would just be left with words on a page. I remember reading a newspaper from beginning to end one day and coming to the obituaries. This old timer had passed from natural causes, and the paper mentioned all that he had accomplished and the family he left behind. I began talking to the empty cell as if I knew this gentleman my whole life, that I had not accomplished shit, and that my obituary would have nothing. I left my family behind, and to some degree many of them left me. My brother would visit when he was in state but my mother, for example, would not humiliate herself with the process they have visitors go through in order to visit.

In the morning I would wake up to grab the breakfast on a tray, that reminded me of food we had in high school, through the slot in the steel door. I would eat regardless of how it tasted because I would get nothing until lunch. After about an hour I would do some push ups, crunches and then shadow box to get my heart rate going. The cop would soon come to the door to ask if I was going to Rec.

"Hell yeah!" I was absolutely going out to the kennels in order to get some air. We called the cages outside where we worked out the kennels because they resembled the pens for dogs. At least out there I could pace around for an hour and let the breeze hit my face.

When the wind would hit my skin, I was back in the forest where we would run around and jump off the rocks. Back in those woods we knew every path and all the trees to climb. Transporting back there was all I wanted to do. To start over. To be a kid again. I would give anything for that.

Soon, however, I would be back in the cell staring at the ceiling. I remember an old timer warned me not to think about my youthful memories for more than thirty seconds. He told me it would kill a man to dwell on the good times he had outside of the walls. So when I felt myself sinking into the past I would jump off that trip as quick as I could.

I continued my existence day in and day out. I was transferred from hole to hole if my behavior was poor, then from unit to unit. I created a life in population. The cycle continued for years.

Nevertheless, a gust hitting my face took me back to my childhood every time.

"Screw you old man!" I would think to myself, ignoring the old timer's advice. If the memories came, I would let them come. I would hold on to them. I would let myself run through the woods and hear us boys laugh. I could see the light through the trees and the smiles on our faces. I could smell those summer days that reached so long into the afternoon. It could have just been thirty seconds. It may have been longer. I didn't care. I was stretched so thin in here that those memories gave me peace. I leaned my face against the kennel and just listened.

EPILOGUE

B rett spent the next seventeen years in the Massachusetts prison system. Simply put this was a very hard time. Brady went on to become a high school art teacher and coach. Technically, this book started half way into Brett's sentence. The two brothers were corresponding by hand-written letters, Brady from Wisconsin and Brett from various prisons in Massachusetts. Brady wrote the stories based on his direct experience and the content that Brett would send him. They did not really gain traction until Brett was finally released May 14, 2015. Finally, not being stalled by snail mail, ups and downs of prison life, moving from facility to facility, coupled with Brett earning his college degree while inside, the project took off. Brett often states that he needed almost the full seventeen years to get his head straight, and if he got out earlier his chances of reoffending were quite high. It was his education and faith that really started to empower him and allowed him to start to turn the corner and truly see a vision for his future.

It is both brothers' hope that this effort will prove valuable to others and help support individuals through their individual struggles. The process of sharing our stories certainly helped us through ours.

Some names and identifying details have been changed to protect the privacy of individuals.

ACKNOWLEDGEMENTS

B rett: I would like to thank my family and close friends who always stood by me and supported me even during troubled times. I owe so much to my faith and certainly my only brother without him none of this would be possible. He allowed me to dream again as if I were a kid starting over.

Brady: I would like to thank everyone in my family for all the support they have given me: my wife, Rhonda, who encouraged me to stay with this project during the early years. Mimi, Kye, Celia, Kara, Uncle Phil, Auntie Ju, Mom, and Mike were all instrumental in their own way. Beth Steffen who helped refine the writing and acted as a great sounding board. I am grateful to many of my friends and coaches who pointed out that I should write some of these stories down and helped encourage me along the way. Of course, Brett because he inspired me with his strength and determination to better himself while inside.

Made in the USA
Middletown, DE
26 September 2021

49085047R00089